EVERYTHING
IS AWFUL

EVERYTHING IS AWFUL

and other observations

MATT BELLASSAI

Keywords PRESS

ATRIA

NEW YORK LONDON TORONTO SYDNEY NEW DELHI

An Imprint of Simon & Schuster, Inc.
1230 Avenue of the Americas
New York, NY 10020

Certain names and characteristics have been changed.

First Keywords Press /Atria Books hardcover edition October 2017

Keywords Press /**ATRIA** BOOKS and colophons are trademarks
of Simon & Schuster, Inc.

For information about special discounts for bulk purchases,
please contact Simon & Schuster Special Sales at 1-866-506-1949
or business@simonandschuster.com.

The Simon & Schuster Speakers Bureau can bring authors to your live
event. For more information or to book an event, contact the Simon
& Schuster Speakers Bureau at 1-866-248-3049 or visit our website at
www.simonspeakers.com.

Interior design by Suet Chong

Manufactured in the United States of America

10 9 8 7 6 5 4 3

Library of Congress Cataloging-in-Publication Data is available.

ISBN 978-1-5011-6649-5
ISBN 978-1-5011-6651-8 (ebook)

For my family.
I blame them for everything.

contents

Everything Is Awful,
and Other Embarrassments   1

On Being an Adult,
or I Have No Idea What I'm Doing   7

On the Trauma of Having (or Not Having) Hair   17

On Being "The Big Guy"   31

Rules for a Totally Healthy and
Not-at-All-Medically-Concerning Lifestyle   41

On My Old and Fragile Body,
or I Feel Bad About My Everything   45

On Near-Death Experiences,
or That Time I Choked on a Taquito   53

A Brief List of Things That I Don't Know   65

On Michigan   69

On the Terrors of Nature   89

On Teenagers and Why They're the Worst   97

On My First 100 Days
as President of the United States   113

On Terrible First Jobs   119

On My Troubled History with Fashion   143

On Being in the Closet, or Why You Should Never
Fall in Love with Your Straight Best Friend   153

On Relationships, or Traits for My Ideal Man   177

On the Sticky Perils of Having a Roommate   181

On Living Alone in New York City   197

On Self-Sufficiency   207

On Keeping a Clean and Tidy Apartment   217

On Not Being the People's Choice   219

Acknowledgments   245

EVERYTHING IS AWFUL, AND OTHER EMBARRASSMENTS

I was six years old when I last peed my pants.

I say this not to brag—although making it over twenty years without pissing my pants is actually quite an accomplishment, to be perfectly honest—but to bare my shame.

I was at my best friend Kenny's house after school, drinking juice boxes and waging war with toy soldiers. You know, six-year-old stuff. As our battle wore on, my body slowly devolved into the cross-legged dance of the six-year-old in distress, writhing to console the mounting pressure of my bladder. As my soldiers fell in the heat of battle, I crept painfully closer to my limit.

I was dressed in my finest outfit for a school assembly earlier that day, some hideous combination of red, black, and white my mother thought was stylish in 1996. In retrospect, that outfit probably deserved to be pissed on. You can't put a budding homosexual in an ill-conceived pattern and expect him not to urinate all over it. Regardless, there I was, standing in front of the toilet (I'd managed, at least, to make it to the bathroom), furiously struggling with the buttons of my fancy six-year-old pants. And yes, my mother chose not only a hideous pattern, but dress pants with *buttons* instead of a zipper, yet another choice that begged for this very outcome. I'd held my composure for as long as I could.

My hands helplessly fumbling at the buttons, I finally succumbed to sweet relief, soaking the plush rug beneath my feet, along with my socks, underwear, and those wretched pants, still buckled around my waist. Some days, when I'm standing in front of a toilet, I can still feel that rug beneath my feet, a moist phantom of my earliest humiliation.

I spent the next twenty minutes silently brooding in that bathroom. They were black pants, after all. Maybe I could get away with acting like this hadn't happened. All I needed to do was spend the next two to three hours in damp agony, and as long as nobody looked too closely or inhaled too deeply, I could escape undetected.

But I spent too long plotting this out, and Kenny's mom knocked on the door.

"Is everything all right in there?" (A question that someone only asks when everything is not all right in there.)

I confessed to the accident, and opened the door in surrender. I thought for a moment maybe she'd stick my nose in it, the way my own mother used to stick our dog's nose in his pee when he pissed where he wasn't supposed to. But she took the carpet from beneath me and handed me a pair of Kenny's old shorts to wear for the rest of our playdate, my very own scarlet letter so that all could bear witness to my shame.

That evening, I left Kenny's house in those shame shorts, carrying my own clothes in a plastic bag, with my head held high, just as Hester walked with her letter before me.

. . .

I couldn't help but think that I somehow deserved what happened.

Earlier that day, my schoolmates and I were eating lunch in our classroom. The gymnasium we'd normally eat in was closed for the assembly, so we were eating at our desks instead, which felt intoxicating, like we were doing something forbidden. Everybody was already hopped up on assembly energy, but now we were especially animated, fidgeting in our seats, screaming across the room, tossing bits of food when the teacher turned her back.

Austin was the boy who sat behind me, a huge lug of a kid, nearly twice as tall as the rest of us and almost twice as thick. If this were a fairy tale, Austin would be the ogre child we'd all run from when he emerged from his swamp. And I'd feel bad about that comparison, but Austin was kind of an asshole, one of those boys who was friendly only until someone better came along, so I treated him with similar respect.

We were drinking from our cartons of milk, those tiny paper boxes that are nearly impossible to open, made of that kind of thin cardboard that gets immediately soggy after the first few sips. Austin was halfway through a long sip when I turned around and made a funny face—my repertoire of humor in first grade was limited to gurgling noises, knock-

knock jokes, and funny faces—and he choked back a mouthful of spittle and milk with a furious scowl.

"Don't!" he screamed with genuine anger. "These are my nice pants! I can't ruin them!"

This made me laugh even harder.

Each time he'd pick up his carton, I'd turn around with my fingers halfway up my nose, my cheeks puffed out, and my eyes crossed, and Austin would cry back, "Stop! If I get milk on my pants, my mom's gonna kill me!"

It went on like this for ten minutes, back and forth, attracting a small audience around us eagerly waiting to see if Austin would ever finish his milk. Until finally, I waited for him to take the largest possible gulp. I turned around at just the right moment with just the right combination of fingers stuffed into the right combination of face holes. Austin lurched forward for a moment to try to stop himself from reacting. And then, all at once, a violent stream of milk exploded from his nose, all down his sweater, and pooled momentarily in his pants before seeping into the fabric.

The audience around us erupted in screams of laughter, and Austin's own outburst turned from a milky chortle to anguish as he stomped away from us, wailing in protest.

There are a few lessons to draw here, the first of which, of course, is that children are terrible human beings, and I was certainly no exception. (Though, in my defense, Austin grew up to be an even bigger dick, and once said, "I'm fat, but at least I'm not fat *and* gay like Matt Bellassai," so I don't regret ruining his dumb pants, and if I could, I'd go back, do it all again, and then smash his stupid face into that puddle of snotty lap milk before it seeped onto his tiny ogre dick.)

Most significantly, though, this was the first time I realized that comedy could be weaponized. I might not have been the fastest or strongest, but I could spin a joke or pull a face, and bring an oafish menace like Austin to his knees. And yes, perhaps I'd have to make myself look like a fool for the sake of a laugh, but at least it was my laugh in the end, even if I ended the day in a pair of someone else's shorts, carrying my own soiled pants and underwear in a plastic Baggie.

. . .

I'm not one of those cool New Yorkers who lunched with Nora Ephron, but I like to pretend that I am. I imagine we would have sat for hours at a café drinking coffees, ordering extra croissants when we'd finished the two we'd each already eaten, and smearing them with extra high-fat butter. We'd have been wearing matching turtlenecks and scarves, discussing which wrinkle-reducing eye creams we'd discovered most recently, or which new dessert shop we would try next, or perhaps, after the sixth croissant, whether Angelina Jolie would ever find love again.

I moved to the Upper West Side in part because I idolized Nora's rendition of it. My studio was only a closet compared to the apartments in the Apthorp, the famous complex down the street where Nora lived for some time. But still, I felt peppy and witty and sophisticated whenever I walked those streets, like a character in one of her movies, waiting for a young, hot Tom Hanks to reach for the same muffin as me at the bakery before sweeping me off my feet and paying off all of my student loan bills. It made my measly New York existence—my piles of takeout containers stacked in the corner, my bathroom without a bathroom door, the stench of burning meats that wrestled its way through the walls from the apartment next door—feel all the more like I was living the life of a scintillating two-time divorcée, a true woman of the city.

Most important, though, living like Nora made it all the easier to find the humor in all those terrible New York moments: discovering mold on the bottom of a breakfast sandwich I'd already half-eaten; falling down an entire subway staircase; dropping an entire container of hot food I'd carefully selected the second I stepped out of the Whole Foods in Union Square.

"Everything is copy," Nora recalls her mother repeating, which she interpreted as a sort of battle cry. "When you slip on a banana peel, people laugh at you," she wrote of her mother's quote, "but when you tell people you slipped on a banana peel, it's your laugh. So you become the hero rather than the victim of the joke."

What follows in this book is a collection of all of my banana-slipping moments, retold here so that I may, perhaps, be the hero and not the victim of my plentiful embarrassments. Consider it a retelling of life's little indignities, all the times I've stood in front of a toilet, desperately grasping at the buttons of my big-boy pants, when everything goes utterly awry, however cosmically deserved.

This book is my Baggie full of pee pants. And I hold it high as the urine-stained hero.

ON BEING AN ADULT, OR I HAVE NO IDEA WHAT I'M DOING

I have no idea what the fuck I'm doing. Like, at all. This morning alone, I hit the snooze button no less than thirteen times before getting out of bed, and let's be real, I only *really* gave in because I had to pee and I figured pissing my sheets would be more trouble than it was worth on a Tuesday afternoon. And yes, before you ask, I have in fact considered peeing my bed rather than standing up and walking fifteen feet to use the toilet, and the day I decide doing laundry is less work than walking to the bathroom is the day we're all in a hell of a lot of trouble. And sure, I managed to put on sweatpants and walk to the deli across the street to order a breakfast sandwich, a muffin, and a chocolate milk, but only before I dragged it all back to my apartment, climbed back into bed, and stuffed it all in my face seconds before falling back asleep for another three and a half hours.

This, my friends, is what I consider a productive day.

Here is my truth. I'm Matt. I'm twenty-six. And I'm terrible at being a functioning, self-sufficient, adult member of society. If they gave out awards for being bad at growing up—like Most Likely to Eat a Frozen Dinner That's Still Frozen Because He Couldn't Wait the Full Four Minutes for the Microwave to Finish—I probably would've won a whole bunch of them by now, but then again, they'd probably make me show up somewhere to accept them, and then I'd have to shower and put on deodorant, and probably wear a bow tie and cuff links, and the thought of doing just one of those things is exhausting enough. Also, I don't even know how to tie a bow tie and I don't really know what cuff links are supposed to do, so my talent for being horrible at adulthood will probably go unrecognized forever. Unless they send me the award in the mail, in which case, I'll totally accept it, but only if I don't have to sign for the package, because I don't like opening the door for the UPS man, since he's usually unreasonably attractive and my eyes are usually still boogered shut from sleeping until four o'clock in the afternoon. But I will absolutely pick it up from the doorway once he leaves.

But I've gotten ahead of myself, which is a thing that tends to happen when you have no idea what you're doing and also you're trying to write a whole fucking book. Apparently writing a book takes a very long time and is not something you can just wait and do the night before it's due, no matter how often it worked in college, 'cause a book is a whole lot longer than those papers you wrote in college, and also nobody is spending money to buy your college paper from the bargain bin at Target, which is where I assume everybody will buy this book.

Whew. Where was I? Oh yes.

The truth is, I'm very bad at growing up, and I always have been. And, like all problems in life, it's most likely my family's fault, or at least it's easiest to just blame it all on them.

Like many babies, I was born with the umbilical cord wrapped around my neck, and I don't technically blame my mother outright, but I do have questions. Sure, it's a perfectly normal thing that happens during labor—it happens in something like one in three childbirths—and most people don't even think twice about it. But in my case, I can't help but wonder whether, on some subconscious level, my mother's body knew exactly what it was doing and simply refused to let go, intent on keeping me in the womb until I became an elderly man and died. Or worse, it was trying to kill me before I had a chance to grow up and write a book that painted her as some kind of overprotective gestapo. Whatever the reason, I survived the attack, blue-faced and bloated, able to breathe on my own. And that was perhaps the first and only time I did anything by myself.

I went on to spend an inordinate amount of my childhood bashfully attached to my mother's pelvis, mostly out of social anxiety, but also because I was raised, from an early age, to fear anything that posed even the mildest of threats. In my mother's worldview, no danger was too small or insignificant to ignore, and my older brother and I were taught to mistrust basically anything that spoke, breathed, or moved.

Riding bikes outside the driveway was a surefire way to end up as roadkill, and roadkill was a surefire way to catch salmonella or rabies or whatever diseases raccoons carried, which we were to safely assume was every disease. Pools of water deeper than puddles were traps sent from heaven to claim little angels. ("A child can drown in an *inch* of water," my mother would often yell. *"An inch."*) And don't even get her started on public parks. Sure, go ahead. Go to the park. Have fun spending the rest of your life cooking meth with the other kids in some guy named Burl's basement. I bet he won't make you a birthday lasagna. In retrospect, I think it's quite possible my mother kept me purposely fat and lazy to make me less attractive to abductors. Go ahead, try stealing my flabby baby boy. Good luck getting him to do shit for you, though. Feeding him alone will cost you a fortune!

And so I grew up thinking every activity was brimming with peril. To Debbie, letting a child onto a trampoline was no less dangerous than arming him with a loaded semiautomatic pistol. A water gun that fired anything more than a sprinkle was the quickest way to lose both eyes. And snow days were not days of glory and amusement, because glory and amusement equaled extremities lost to frostbite. "If the snow is too dangerous for you to go to school in," she told us, "then it's definitely too dangerous to play in."

Now, my mother was by no means a doomsayer who forced us to live in some bunker and bide our time until the nuclear apocalypse burnt us all to hell (though we did stock up on canned goods before Y2K, but that was just common sense). In fact, my mother freely encouraged us to go outside—as long as we stayed within six to ten inches of the front door at all times—and we were given all the trappings of midwestern suburban kid life, like scooters, big wheels, pogo sticks, and skateboards—and we could do anything we wanted with them, as long as anything didn't include riding, jumping, running, brisk walking, or moving.

I know, of course, that all of this worrying came only from a place of love. My mother likes to remind me that I was a miracle baby, because her uterus had been almost entirely removed before she became pregnant with me, and doctors told her the likelihood of conceiving another child was basically next to impossible. Which is all to say that I was not a miracle, but what they call a big, fat accident. But still. I was her precious baby boy, handed to her by Jesus himself. I grew up, in other words, being what psychiatrists might later diagnose as "hopelessly coddled into emotional and physical dependency," which is just fancy talk for "loved too much and fucked up because of it."

By the time I was old enough to go to preschool, I'd already become so terrified of the grown-up world that I literally refused to get out of the car on the first day of school. When my mother came around the car to open the door for me, I'd scurried up to the driver's seat, locked all the doors, and sat steadfast in nonviolent protest. If I'd had the stamina, I would still be there today. They managed eventually to lure me out with the promise of sugar and gifts, but once we were inside, I refused to be put down, and dug into the thick of my mother's arm while three grown adults attempted to peel me from her. This happened every morning for the first week of preschool, until they finally broke me.

Of course, I can't entirely blame my mother for teaching me to fear the world, in part because she will read this book, and if she's made it this far, I'm sure she's already pissed, and I have no doubt she's already plotting her own revenge memoir just to publish every embarrassing detail of my entire existence in excruciating specificity. But also, I have to be fair. Because Michael Jackson is also to blame.

Now I know what you're thinking, and no, I never had to go to court and point at a doll and I'm almost positive I've never been to Neverland Ranch. But Michael Jackson ruined my childhood nonetheless. Let me explain.

When I was somewhere around two or three years old, I was minding my own business, probably playing with my Mr. Potato Head in peace, when Michael Jackson's "Thriller" came on the television. This was 1993, it had been a full decade since "Thriller" was first released, but they only showed three things on TV in the nineties—*The Oprah Winfrey Show*, TV shows about black teenagers going to live with their aunties and uncles in Bel Air, and thirteen-minute-long music videos—and "Thriller" fell into at least two of those categories. For whatever reason, my mother thought it would be a good idea for me, her three-year-old infant baby child, to see this video with my own two innocent baby eyes. She beckoned me over from Mr. Potato Head and innocently said, "Look, Matthew. Watch the man turn into a big doggie." She figured, I guess, that I was three, and my interests included dogs, bright jackets, and effeminate men, so maybe I'd enjoy watching Michael Jackson turn into what she affectionately believed to be a large, kind puppy.

Of course, if you've seen Michael Jackson's "Thriller," you know that this is a wild mischaracterization of what happens in the video. Dogs are friendly and they are nice and they lick your face. Michael Jackson does not turn into a dog. Michael Jackson turns into a jagged-fanged, yellow-eyed, contorted-faced werewolf who literally rips a girl to shreds. And my mother made me watch that shit. The second his eyes turned into angry yellow slits, I screamed like he had personally burst through our front door, and I leapt headfirst into my mother's uterus (or what was left of it), refusing to reemerge for nearly three days. Some nights, I close my eyes, and I still see his face.

And perhaps I would've forgotten this event, had it not been for my brother, who purchased a rubber werewolf mask days later, just to chase me around the house while I screamed for mercy.

To make matters even worse, not long after this, my older cousin Nick tried to scare me into obedience with a story about a clown named Pennywise who stole insubordinate children in their sleep and forced them to work in underground labor camps. It didn't matter that this was merely a bastardized version of a Stephen King novel. I believed it outright, and spent four straight nights without sleep, shaking uncontrollably, fearful that closing my eyes guaranteed my immediate kidnapping.

This is all to say that I entered adolescence scarred not just by my mother, but also by my brother, my cousin, Pennywise the child-stealing clown, and Michael Jackson himself. It should be no surprise that I'm fucked up. I spent most of early childhood fully expecting every person I met to transform into a wild-eyed beast who would kill me in my sleep, if they could get to me before the clown forced me into hard labor.

Eventually, of course, I grew up, and those fears went away. But the fun thing about fears is that they're easily replaced with a bunch of new fears that are just as believable and overwhelming. Don't drive a car faster than 10 mph, because you will crash and we won't even be able to identify your body. Don't drink alcohol before you're twenty-one, or your liver will tell your brain to become an alcoholic, and you'll spend the rest of your life in rehab, where they don't even get all the TV channels. Don't get on airplanes because airplanes are the number-one travel method of terrorists, and if the terrorists don't kill you, it doesn't even matter, because the plane is gonna crash on its own anyway.

It's a miracle I make it outside of the house at all.

So here we are. I'm now twenty-six, which is the age at which people start to assess whether you have your shit together, or at least whether you have the mental and physical capacity for one day getting your shit together. It's the age at which people start categorizing your laziness as less of an endearing quirk and more of a problem the government will have to solve one day. It's when people start to wonder how long you really have before shit goes entirely off the rails and you end up as one of those people on the evening news who managed to live unnoticed in the basement of a Staten Island Burger King, and when the reporter asks you why you've been living down here all these years, you ramble about trampolines and snow days and Michael Jackson and a demon clown.

It's the age at which you should know what the fuck you're doing, regardless of how much the world fucked you up.

And yet, I have no idea what the fuck I'm doing. I don't date. I don't drive. I don't eat right. I don't exercise. I don't cook. I don't clean. I don't know how to dress myself. And I can't remember where I left my remote, which should be the least of my concerns, but somehow it's the most upsetting.

Now, I know what you're thinking. "Matt, none of us know what the fuck we're doing with our lives and all of us have problems and we're all just meaningless sacks of meat wandering aimlessly around a rock that's hurtling through space, and eventually that rock will slam into the sun and the universe will explode and none of this will mean a damn thing." Which is true. But also I can't help but feel like the Italian boy behind the bodega counter is judging me every time I show up at three in the morning to buy a pint of mint chocolate chip gelato. He doesn't seem to care that the sun is gonna melt the earth one day. All he seems to care about is that I only need one plastic spoon and no bag, because he knows I'm popping the lid off this thing the second I walk out the door.

So yes. I have no idea what I'm doing. Today, I went outside. I ate a sandwich and a muffin. I drank a chocolate milk. I took a long nap. And it was a productive day.

ON THE TRAUMA OF HAVING (OR NOT HAVING) HAIR

I was born with a freakish amount of hair. Or so they tell me. I don't really like to talk about the day I was born, because it's the first and only time I touched a vagina, and I like to pretend I have a clean record. And yes, technically my picture got taken right after I slid out, but you can't really tell how much hair a baby has from a picture taken seconds after it emerges from amniotic juices. Based on the sole surviving photograph I have of that day, whatever hair I had was caked in what looks like thick strawberry jam, except it wasn't strawberry jam, it was bits of placenta, because they don't even dry you all the way off before they snap the picture that will one day end up on your birthday cakes. They should really wait until the placenta dries and flakes off before they take the picture.

So no, I don't know exactly how much hair I had when I was born, but my mother likes to brag that I had a lot of it. Which is kind of a weird thing to gloat about, if you ask me.

I don't like seeing a single strand of hair on my dinner plate. I can't imagine an entire ball of it growing in my uterus for nine months and emerging from my body, sentient and screaming for food, and then being like, "Yeah, I made that. And now I'm gonna let it live in my house for twenty years." In fact, in eighth-grade health class, that most sacred of American public school institutions, wherein children are first informed that hair will start growing from places previously unheard of in life, I distinctly remember watching *The Miracle of Birth*, a horrid documentary in which a Wisconsin woman with a bad perm is freed of an alien that's been swelling in her abdomen. It astounds me, to this day, that we force thirteen-year-olds to watch a woman giving birth on VHS tape and consider this sexual education. I barely even knew what a vagina looked like on a regular day, let alone the day a screaming mass of hair decides to claw out of it. But that's not the point. The point is, I had to watch that mess, and I remember viscerally gagging during the scene when It Happens, not because of the miracle of it all, but because of the sheer amount of hair that's involved in the whole thing. Babies are covered in it. Vaginas are covered in it. I tried to avoid looking at it straight on by peering above my glasses and letting my blurry vision dull my ability to see what was happening, but I still remember, fuzzy eyesight be damned, the angry, throbbing ball of fur emerging from between that screaming woman's legs. It was like watching a ball of rats crawl through the hole of a sewer drain. During a mudslide. (To make matters worse, my health teacher—who also happened to be my gym teacher, my history teacher, and the football coach, because American public schools are masters of efficiency—was a widower whose wife died in childbirth because, by some freak medical anomaly, a *hair* got into her bloodstream when she was in labor and *murdered* her to death. I'm not making this up. The bulk of my sexual education came from a man whose life was literally ruined by hair. And that's not even mentioning the pictures of hairy, gonorrhea-stricken genitals he showed us on the first day of class.)

I guess my mother didn't know that hair kills, or maybe she was happy simply knowing that my hairy ass didn't murder her on the way out, because she *still* talks about walking down the hospital hallway to the tiny deli counter they keep the babies in and being able to spot me right away, my wispy ginger hair blowing in the wind. Little did she know, that wispy ginger hair would go on to ruin my life.

This may go without saying, but I don't like hair. Hair is disgusting, and a generally terrible inconvenience. It collects grease and dirt and particles of old, crusty food. It gathers in clumps, a unit of measurement that has never been used to describe anything good in this world. (You know what else gathers in clumps? Herpes.) It clogs my shower drain. It mixes with toothpaste to congeal on the sides of my sink. It piles up in thickets beneath my furniture and comes scurrying out like tumbleweeds the second I have someone over. And let's be real, it's far outlasted its evolutionary purpose. Cavemen needed hair to keep warm and, I can only imagine, given their relative abundance of free time, to have something to aimlessly braid between hump sessions. But let's face it, I have central heating and the Internet, so whatever value hair added to the cave people's lives seems to have been generally satisfied. Apparently, anthropologists think humans lost our cave hair when we gained the ability to walk on two legs and needed to better regulate our body temperatures for long-distance runs. Considering I have never, and will never, run any long distances in my life, once again, hair's purpose is unnecessary.

Worst of all, hair is needy. My hair has never been longer than a few inches, and yet, I've used approximately every product ever made in the entirety of history to attempt to wield power over it, a list that grows every year as they invent new ways to get me to spend my money on chemicals. In the nineties, there was just gel, mousse, or hairspray, and you put it on your frosted tips, and that was the end of it. But now, hell has expanded, and there are pastes, pomades, waxes, putties, glues, clays, creams *and* crèmes (difference unclear), lotions, oils, exfoliating scalp treatments, grooming serums, and, I'm not fucking around with you on this one, quicksand. And we haven't even gotten to the endless varieties of conditioners—the function of which I still don't entirely understand—and shampoos, which you can now apparently use in dry form, a luxury I refuse to believe actually works. And this is just the hair on your head! There are the creams, foams, and tonics you're supposed to use *before* you shave, and the moisturizers, oils, and lotions you're supposed to use *after* you shave, and of course, you have to get a shaver, or actually two shavers, unless you want to shave the hair around your mouth with the same instrument you use to shave the hair around your testicles. Oh, and also one of those weird-shaped shavers that go up your nostrils and inside your ears, and possibly one of those contraptions you can use to shave the hair on your back. And tweezers for everything in between. And despite all of this, my hair *still* looks like it belongs on the head of a politician who tries to solicit sex in an airport bathroom. (Oh, and don't even get me *started* on the TSA's crusade against hair products on airplanes. What havoc could I possibly wreak on an airplane with a bottle of ultra-firm holding spray? Answer me that, TSA people! You know who had awful hair? Osama bin Laden. By making me throw away my conditioner, you're just playing into his master plan. This is what he wanted.)

In fairness, I am a man, and my struggle with hair is but a fraction of the battle that women are expected to wage daily. My haircuts cost less than a McDonald's value meal, and theoretically, I could just decide to stop caring about it one day, and everybody would assume I was preparing for my breakout role as Guy Who Sniffs Paint Behind a Denny's. And of course, as a white guy, my hair carries none of the cultural baggage that people of color reckon with every day. Nobody has tried to reach out and touch my hair on the train, and generally speaking, nobody has questioned how often I wash it. All things considered, I have it relatively easy.

But still, I don't like hair. I don't like the hair on my head, or the hair in my armpits, or the hair that grows in all the other places that hair has absolutely no reason growing other than to serve as itchy, sweaty decoration. I hate that I have to wash it, and condition it, and cut it, and style it, and make sure there are no bugs making babies in it. I hate that I can't get rid of it because my skull is the shape of a peeled yam and my skin is oily and if I went fully bald, my scalp would look like an angry jack-o'-lantern. I hate that I have to brush it every time I leave my apartment because I look like I'm plotting to steal Christmas if I don't. And I hate that it has had the audacity to make me care for it—to grow it and water it and pet it every day for almost three loving decades—and now it's finally deciding to go away, strand by strand, and refusing to come back.

Perhaps it finally caught on to the fact that I don't like it very much, and made the unilateral decision to abandon me en masse, but that's typical hair behavior. It gives you hell and demands it all, and then leaves the second you start getting used to it.

My dependency on hair started before I can even remember. I was born with the comb-over of a televangelist, and forces beyond my control decided to make this the only haircut that would ever work with my body type and facial features long before I could possibly have any say in the matter. For one disastrous week in 1999, I attempted to take matters into my own hands and experimented with a center part, and my entire life nearly fell to pieces. The order of the universe continues to depend on my hair being parted in the same spot it was first parted by Moses himself, which is exactly 30 percent across my scalp, from left to right.

Every morning of my childhood, for as long as I could remember, I would run up to my mother with a long comb and a spray bottle full of water. She would wet my hair until I could feel the tiny droplets dripping down my temples, and then part it in two or three short strokes, always in the same spot. Then, while it was still damp, she would pick up an oversized aerosol can and thoroughly douse my head in a gallon of megahold hairspray until my hair turned into virtual stone. I spent most of my adolescence with the shiny, immovable hair of a pin-striped eighties stockbroker. In almost every picture of me as a child, it's almost impossible to tell I had ginger hair at all, because it was covered in so much product, it looked like the color of wet clay, and had the stiffness of titanium. And it soon became part of my public identity. Classmates would gather around me on the playground during recess and take turns knocking on my hair like they were knocking on a slab of concrete. On weekends, the local blacksmith would come to our house and use my hair to forge wrought iron into various decorative metal fixtures. And I once won a battering contest against a very formidable ram.

Of course, as with any well-publicized strength, vulnerabilities were right around the corner. And my enemies knew this well.

My brother, who is six years older than I am, had plenty of time to reckon with his hair journey long before I came along. A true child of the nineties, he was far more adventurous with using hair as a form of expressing inner angst, and cycled through countless iterations of spikes, colored tips, and bleaches, including a brief foray into pink hair dye that nearly tore our family apart. (He insisted on dying his head the color of chewed bubble gum. Mom and Dad insisted that any such action was akin to joining one of those cults where you have to drown a kitten to get in. He did it anyway. My parents had to kill a cat just to prove their point.)

Now, many years later, he's given up on taming his hair entirely, opting instead for a shaggy, unkempt mop and an unwieldy beard. He looks very much like the kind of person who goes hunting for game with his bare hands and has bitten directly into a still-beating deer heart. In many ways, the disparity in our hair choices is emblematic of the differences we exhibited more broadly: he preferred the more rebellious, Hot Topic–inspired way of life, and I preferred the more genteel lifestyle of a door-to-door vacuum-cleaner salesman. To say we did not particularly mesh would be an understatement. And yet, I insisted on being included in whatever activities he partook in, per my contractual duties as younger sibling.

When he inevitably exploded (which was often, I was very annoying), no retaliatory target was as appealing as my hair. It was, after all, the thing I seemingly cared most about, and representative of my general stodginess and infuriating nature. If I were a terrorist looking to inflict the most symbolic damage on my annoying eight-year-old self, I would've chosen my hair, too. By then, I'd learned how to wet it, comb it, and spray it myself, and spent a considerable amount of time in the bathroom every morning getting every strand just right, so as to be best prepared for my daily regimen of aggressive pestering. My hair was precious to me.

I don't remember what I did to piss him off this particular time. We were outside in the middle of summer. I might've taken his bike or stepped on his foot or sprayed his back too many times with the water gun I'd gotten for my birthday. But whatever it was, it sent him into a wild-eyed rage. He came at me, I screamed at an octave only birds could hear, he grabbed me by the shoulders and, taking a deep breath, spit the wad of chewing gum he'd been chomping on directly onto my scalp.

Now you'd think, given the amount of hairspray I'd covered it with, that my hair would've been protected by a sort of chemical force field, that the gum would've hit the hard surface and bounced right off, and I'd have been free to continue my pestering emboldened by my brother's failed revenge plot. But you'd be fucking wrong. Because of course it didn't bounce right off. It fucking stuck. Because that's what gum does.

I figured, at first, that if it had stuck only lightly, I could reach in and pluck it right out, like picking a grape out of a shag carpet. (This is the best metaphor I could think of, and I'm sorry. Backup options included: "like fetching a hard-boiled egg from a patch of weeds," and "like fishing a piece of orange chicken from a pile of hay.") Naturally, my attempts to pick it out merely exacerbated the situation, and I ran wailing to my mother, whose own attempts proved even less effective, perhaps because my body was convulsing in dramatic sobs as her fingers spread the gum into more and more clumps. If you've ever tried cleaning shit out of a dog's ass hair, you know exactly what we were dealing with here. Every time you try to wipe, the dog moves, and the shit somehow multiplies, until it has spread into a far larger, even shittier patch of destruction.

I'm sure there are plenty of mommy bloggers today who know the exact mixture of peanut butter, vegetable oil, and angel tears you need to get gum out of a kid's hair without resorting to the nuclear option, but this was 1998 and all we had was a dial-up connection. We weren't about to wait thirty minutes for the computer to connect to the Internet so we could figure out how to get gum out of hair the fancy way.

So, having protested that I would rather live with the mangled, patchy hairstyle of an off-brand clown than shave it all off, my mother proceeded to perform spot surgery and literally hacked the gum from my head until every sticky trace had been excised. We spent the next several days traveling from one suburban Supercuts to another. At every stop, my mother would spin me around, point to the spot where she'd taken an axe to my skull, and look expectantly at each stylist to see who could conjure enough magic to make me whole again. But the desecration had been too deep. My crown had been broken. And there was no fixing the damage that had been inflicted on my soul.

It probably grew back in like a week, because kids' hair grows like mold on old bread. But I learned a valuable lesson that day. Hair can never be trusted, no matter how religiously you wash it, condition it, wet it, part it, and hairspray it. The second it gets the chance, it'll gleefully ruin your entire goddamn life. One chopped gummy patch at a time.

. . .

As I got older and the children who once knocked on my hardened hair grew into judgmental teenagers eager to pounce on anything even slightly unordinary, I abandoned my hairspray in favor of the more relaxed, no-frills vibe of a thirteen-year-old with split ends. Which is to say, I spent most of high school with hair that had the consistency of straw because it had been blow-dried to within an inch of its life every single morning. But it worked for me.

Of course, my hair, knowing full well that I'd found some sense of equilibrium in life, couldn't let well enough alone, and began conspiring with my hormones to bring life new hellish meaning. Hair began appearing in places it had never been before, bringing with it fresh new odors and itchiness and discomfort.

As a Bellassai, I'm at the end of a long line of Italian men (and women) with body hair thicker than lush forest moss. I used to lie awake at night and wonder why we couldn't have turned out like the oiled, hairless men in the Dolce&Gabbana ads. I'm sure *they* never had to shave their necks beneath the collars of their shirts, or tweeze obsessively between their eyebrows, or brush the fur on their toe knuckles. I bet *their* shower drains didn't look like they were trying to flush the decaying carcass of a trampled wildebeest.

When my father took off his shirt, it looked like he'd covered himself in glue and rolled around the floor of a veterinarian's office. I used to wonder how he ever fully dried himself off after swimming in the pool. And this is what I inherited.

My hair didn't grow normally, though. The hair on my face didn't all decide to arrive at once, at the same, even length. It grew one at a time, starting with one very ambitious strand that grew from the dead center of my cheek and coiled before I'd noticed it. It was long enough that a girl at school reached out and physically plucked it from my face, before she said, "Awww, look who's becoming a man," an event that continues to haunt me to this day, but mostly because she had no idea if maybe I wanted to keep that whisker as a souvenir or if I'd been growing it out as an experiment.

When I eventually had enough hair to shave, I pressed way too hard with the electric shaver, and had my first lesson in the searing pain of razor burn, which is just another one of hair's backhanded gifts. Hair ushers you into adulthood, welcomes you with the new responsibilities of maturity, and then, when you finally muster the confidence to deal with it, takes a layer of your skin clean off on its way out.

· · ·

Sometime around my twenty-second birthday was when I first realized that the hair on my head was beginning to thin. I noticed it, as you notice most things in life, in the reflection of my head on the blank screen of my phone. At first I thought it might just be the angle—nobody looks like they have much hair when they're looking at themselves from beneath a triple chin. But when I brought up my grip, I saw that the hair at the front of my head seemed just a little less thick than usual.

My hair had always been thick, thick enough that the stylist at Supercuts was forced to use thinning shears just to work with it, but perhaps because of the amount of chemicals I'd put in my hair since birth, or the aggressive way I combed it every morning, or my general lack of a healthy diet and exercise regimen (but probably not), it was undoubtedly starting to grow thinner. My mother blamed the woman at Supercuts for her indiscriminate use of the thinning shears, but I suspect she was just angry I'd started going to a salon rather than have her cut my hair in the laundry room with the same scissors she used to groom the dog, and was looking for a reason to prove me wrong. She had cut my hair until I was nearly twenty years old, and the betrayal she felt when I finally announced I'd be going to a strip-mall beauty parlor reverberated for months. She *still* blames those Supercuts thinning shears for my receding hairline, despite the fact that it's receding in the same fashion as my father's and his father's before him, in what some might call a pattern of male baldness.

It's been a handful of years since then, and I'm glad to say that I still have a fair amount of hair on my head. (And, for the curious, a thriving amount of hair everywhere else.)

But here is hair's final twist of the knife. I'm now an adult gay man, at a point when hair is of premium importance in life. After all, in the gay community, for better or worse, hair defines everything. It is virtually the single most ubiquitous characteristic in the gay taxonomy: there are twinks, bears, otters, cubs, wolves—all defined one way or another by the presence or lack of hair. And I fit neatly into none of those categories, which means if I ever do porn, they won't even know what part of the website to put me in. (For the record, if I had to categorize myself, I probably most closely resemble a bear, but like Paddington, because I always keep my clothes on, so the porn thing will have to be artsy, like for guys who get off on watching other guys eat meatball sandwiches.)

The gay community has had a long obsession with grooming, and for many, a proper, professional gay needs to be waxed, shaved, and styled to perfection—all before getting out of bed. Beards, which are now the defining symbol of gay hotness, should be trimmed and shaped to emulate no less than the Spartans themselves. And of course, manscaping is an absolute must, and body hair of any kind should be expunged, besides perfect, decorative topiaries above the genitals, beneath the armpits, and along the arms. Failure to meet any of these specifications will result in the immediate destruction of one's gay card.

So now, with a mop of thinning ginger fur, I must endure hair's latest streak of sabotage. It wasn't enough to plague me through childhood, to cast a dark and itchy shadow over puberty, or to bring home bugs that one time we went swimming in an unfamiliar lake. It looms over me still, now armed with the sharpened knife of the gays' piercing judgment, staring back at me in the mirror every morning with an ever wispier glare.

Maybe I'll just wear wigs.

ON BEING
"THE BIG GUY"

I first discovered I was fat the day I no longer fit beneath the bed. I was playing hide-and-seek, and this was my go-to spot, mostly because it was dark and quiet and I could pick at the fuzzies that dangled from the bottom of the box spring. But this day, I couldn't quite squeeze my stomach beneath the metal frame. To be fair, my family had very thick carpeting and very short bed frames, so the space between bed and floor was very difficult to squeeze into to begin with. But still. One day I fit, and the next day I didn't.

It's a harsh way for a kid to discover he's fat, especially when there's a kid in the next room counting down from ten, which is a really short amount of time to both process your newfound fatness and also find another equally sufficient hiding spot. There should really be a hide-and-seek rule for a scenario like this. Like "The hiding countdown may be extended from ten seconds to twenty-five years in the event of an existential crisis of the body. Adjust accordingly and may God have mercy on your portly soul." But let's face it, the rules of hide-and-seek were never that solid to begin with.

In my parents' eyes, I was never fat, I was just a "growing boy" with a healthy appetite who needed to eat whatever he wanted in order to grow big and strong. Never mind that I went up three pant sizes each year, or that I could barely run across the backyard without suffering severe stomach cramps, or that I was developing my own petite little boy breasts. This is what happened to all little boys. We'd grow into it, the logic went. For now, eat your burgers and fries (read: protein and vegetables), because little boys need all the nutrients they can get.

You can pinpoint the year I got fat by looking at my school pictures. You can clearly see the year my metabolism realized it was in for a lifetime of grueling hard work and gave the fuck up. In first grade, I had discernible cheekbones and the hint of a jawline; by second grade, puffy red cheeks and the beginnings of a double chin.

The thing is, I've always loved to eat. I mean, yes, technically, everybody likes to eat. We're sort of biologically engineered to like it or we die. I just happened to like eating beyond the point where eating was necessary for survival and into the point where you're only stuffing your face with cold mac and cheese because there's nothing better to do at three in the morning on a Tuesday. It didn't help that I was also generally averse to any and all types of physical activity, and preferred watching reruns of *Three's Company* with a bag of potato chips indoors over running around with the neighborhood kids outside.

My family never had an unhealthy relationship with food, but we weren't exactly the picturesque vision of American vigor. We're midwesterners, which means we liked food and we ate it more than we did anything else. Sure, we never had the best diets, but never for lack of trying. We ate our vegetables, if "eat your vegetables" meant "eat your gravy-covered mashed potatoes and broccoli casserole." We ate healthy snacks, if healthy snacks included a heaping bowl of sugary breakfast cereal as a midnight treat before bedtime. And we sustained consistent, stable diets, if consistency included being regulars at the local Dairy Queen. Seriously, we could walk into that place and leave with extra-large Brownie Blizzards without having to say a single word. Plus, our diets were economical. Whenever Oreos were on sale at the grocery store, my mom stocked up like we were preparing for the zombie apocalypse and the only means of survival was hidden between layers of cookies and cream.

We also weren't a particularly active family, and the activities we did participate in usually revolved around food. The year McDonald's released those Beanie Baby Happy Meal toys, my mom drove us to every McDonald's franchise in the greater Chicago area, until we tracked down every last piece-of-garbage Beanie Baby in the set. (Maybe we didn't have problems with food. But we did have problems with Beanie Babies.) And yes, obviously, we ordered Happy Meals at every stop, but only because you had to order the meal in order to get the toys. Still, we ended up with enough burgers to last for breakfast, lunch, and dinner for the next three years.

Meanwhile, I was aware I was growing larger and I felt inferior because of it. My brother, chastised for the litany of insults and taunts he frequently lobbed my way, resorted instead to calling me "big guy," which was, technically speaking, not actually an insult like "fatso" or "tubby," but a fairly benign (and accurate) description of my growing frame. "Nice one, big guy," he'd say whenever he wanted to see me angry. "Having a snack there, big guy?" And I'd stomp my chubby feet and blow air through my nose and demand that my mom make him call me something less insulting, like "four eyes" or "baby Hitler."

It didn't help, though, that he was right. I was big, and getting bigger. In the winter of 1999, my brother and I went sledding on the hill across the street from our house. I squeezed into the pair of overall snow pants I'd worn the year before, except this year, it felt like a corset. I could barely fasten the zipper along my bust and stomach. I could feel my lungs straining against my gallbladder. I managed to cover myself securely enough, but the second we got outside, I bent over to position my sled, and those snow pants ripped open right along the butt with a deafening tear. The white stuffing from inside the pants gushed out like I was shitting dust. "Good going, big guy," my brother yelled as I ran back to the house, covering my gaping ass in humiliation.

It wasn't until high school that I began to feel serious shame for my weight, beyond the boyish taunts of childhood. By that time, I'd started to succumb to all the usual changes that plague young high school boys. Things were reshaping, hair was growing, limbs were extending. And high school was when I joined the rest of adult America and started taking antidepressants, which made my fleshy man boobs even fleshier. (Which is a legitimate and cruel side effect of antidepressants. Oh, you're feeling sad because you're growing up all chubby? Here, take some meds that'll make you *need a man bra*.) Until then, of course, I could hide my girth beneath a heavy T-shirt or a jacket. The only people who had seen my bare stomach or thighs were my family, and even then, I'd kept my weight as concealed as I could. But high school locker rooms are where insecurities go to be exposed. It was the first time I could see the raw evidence of my body compared to other boys, how my stomach, which hung just slightly over the seam of my underwear, was nowhere near as flat or as toned as everyone else's, that my muscles (or whatever there was of them) were hidden beneath a doughy layer of padding, that my thighs jiggled slightly more, and that I needed a thicker T-shirt.

It's also the first time I started noticing men's bodies as more than just bodies, but as objects of desire. Young gay kids are plagued with the dual struggle of wanting to be with the bodies that haunt us and wanting to be like them, those desires often irrevocably tangled up in one another. I didn't know if I was watching the other shirtless boys because I wanted to look like them, or because I liked the way they looked, or both. I didn't know if the shame I felt was about my own body or my own desires. And the confusion made it all not worth thinking about at all. And so, I ignored my own body. I ignored its growing size. I ignored that the food I was eating was related to the rate my body was expanding.

And so, I brought my weight and its baggage to college, where I discovered dining hall waffles and new depths of stress and caffeine and alcohol and more mature, cut bodies and eating burgers at midnight and ramen noodles and boys with cute, muscled thighs and brownies from the dessert station and chugging cheap beer. I gained the freshman fifteen for four students all on my own, because there was too much to worry about besides my weight. And my body escaped me.

Meanwhile, I came out as gay (but not as fat) in 2011 and started learning how much gay culture favors the thin and the fit and the muscled. It's the first time I went to a gay club and saw people who were gay like me, which was at once liberating and suppressive. It was the first time I saw how important it was for gay people to look like some unattainable ideal. "Look at all these thin people being thin together" was my most searing thought, and part of the reason why I never seriously tried dating after that night. Dating felt too much like putting myself on sale at a deli counter, to be picked alongside finer, shinier pieces of beef. I felt too much like a wedge of ham surrounded by beautiful cuts of prime rib.

That summer, I decided to try to take control and joined the gym across the street from our house. And if you're thinking, "The gym was *just* across the street this whole time and you didn't go before then?"—yes, that's exactly where it was, but any gym that was not directly beneath my body at any given moment might as well have been in another country. But, motivated by the insecurity of my newfound gayness, I walked over to the gym one morning, paid the necessary seven-million-dollar membership fee, signed my name in blood, and committed myself to looking like Matthew McConaughey by the end of the summer.

Of course, that dream lasted for about forty-five minutes, which remain some of the worst minutes of my entire life, for about a thousand reasons.

I mean, going to the gym isn't a particularly pleasant experience to begin with, because all gyms are terrible, even the good ones. They smell like hot milk and old rags and garbage bags full of sweaty rubber. There's always a grown man in the corner grunting wildly at his own reflection, a teenager running dangerously fast on the treadmill so that you're scared to go anywhere near him, and an old woman who insists on making flirtatious eye contact with you during the entirety of your workout, and you know it's flirtatious because she's constantly licking her lips. Plus, none of the machines come with instructions, so you may very well spend an entire hour pulling on what you think is part of a machine that trains your shoulders but is actually just a piece of duct tape attached to a laundry machine that nobody told you not to touch. Gyms, generally speaking, are designed to humiliate and terrify you into emotional vulnerability so that gym employees can get you to buy things you don't actually want or need.

Already emotionally distressed, I was an easy target for their hunt. Gym employees, like prowling lionesses, can detect weakness, and they smelled my fragility from miles away. They pounced the second I limped through the front door.

"Welcome," a man with dazzling white teeth and a tight T-shirt shouted when I walked up to the front desk. "Would you like to start off your membership with a free personal training session?" This is the gym predator's trademark maneuver.

Determined as I was for McConaughey-like results in less than ten weeks, and inclined as I am to accept any free thing that is offered to me, I accepted.

"Wonderful," he said. "Let's set you up with a trainer." And he whistled over a man he introduced as Tim, who led me deep in the gym, far enough away so that I could no longer see the front doors or the light that poured in from outside.

Tim, like most gym trainers, had too many muscles, which doesn't seem like it would be a problem in theory, but in the real world, it's like looking at a snake swallow a bag of onions. An approximate foot shorter than I was, Tim seemed to compensate for his height by adding thirty pounds of muscle for every inch he felt he lacked, which made him almost as wide as he was tall. Unprompted, he demonstrated the thickness of his chest by raising his fists in front of his face and struggling to make his forearms touch. This display was apparently meant to impress me, but all I could wonder was whether he could comfortably reach his own penis. I can only conclude, based on his abundance of unspent testosterone, that he could not.

Wasting no further time on verbal introductions, Tim immediately launched into barking orders, which I was expected to wordlessly obey: jumping jacks, push-ups, sit-ups, with no break in between, one after the other, all while Tim screamed what he believed to be encouragements in my face.

"Push harder," he yelled through spittle. "We haven't even gotten started yet!" And yet my muscles were already sending every distress signal they could muster to my brain, shaking wildly and burning hot.

Sensing my waning energy, Tim continued bleating.

"Who's the hottest girl in your class?" he shouted. And my brain, at least the parts of it that weren't preoccupied with keeping the rest of my body from shutting down entirely, began to whir.

In normal circumstances, I would've had the time and patience to address this question properly. Perhaps I would have mustered the energy to explain to Tim that sometimes boys like putting their penises inside other boys' penises. Perhaps I could've explained that I couldn't name the hottest girl in my class if you'd paid me a thousand dollars, but I could rank the hottest fifty boys by ten different criteria, including arms, abs, butts, calves, bulges, pecs, hair, jawlines, smiles, and thighs (the top of which in each category respectively, I could've easily told him, was Pat, Tom, Pat, Ryan, Steven K., Steven R., Jeremy, Kevin, Pat, and Bradley, Pat being the clear and obvious winner).

In my distress, however, my brain could muster none of these explanations, and in a panic, between jumping jacks, my lungs straining hard enough to breathe and speak at the same time, I shouted, "Amanda!"

Tim gave an approving grunt, as if to say, "Ugh, she sounds hot," based solely on the name that I'd shouted under duress.

"What's your favorite part about her?" he continued while I whimpered further.

"Her butt, I guess," I said without even thinking about it, my lungs nearly collapsed at this point.

"Ugh," Tim grunted again, as if I were describing a juicy steak. "Is it big? Do you like her big, fat ass?"

"Yes," I was shouting back at him between jumping jacks. "I love it . . . I love her big, fat ass."

He laughed knowingly, as if to say, "I knew it! This is what all guys come in here for. To do jumping jacks for some girl named Amanda and her big fat ass."

And content with discovering my secret, Tim let me stop.

At the end of our session, Tim gave me a pat on the back. "A few more of these sessions, and we'll have Amanda noticing you in no time."

I smiled feebly, and when he walked away, I limped as fast as I could to the door, and never went to that place again.

.   .   .

That summer, despite my heterosexual fiasco with Tim, I still lost thirty pounds. I counted calories. I went down two waist sizes. And yet, I felt no different. I went back to college and gained it all back.

Then I moved to New York, where something changed. I still ate too much. I still drank too much. After all, New York is a city where you can easily order a slice of chocolate cake at three in the morning (and I have, and I'll do it again), where you can have groceries delivered directly to your apartment and nobody has to see you putting five packages of chocolate chip cookies into a shopping cart that's already full of breads and sugar and fat. Indeed, the entire culture of New York City is built upon meeting people for dinner, for drinks, for appetizers. Bodegas are open all night in case the desire for a pint of mint chocolate chip ice cream strikes at midnight.

But New York is also where I learned that being fat does not equal being ashamed. It's a thin city, that much is true. But it's also a diverse city that celebrates its differences more than it's willing to admit. And there I learned that being fat is not a moral judgment. That carrying extra weight does not mean carrying extra baggage. That being fat is not always a choice. That it's important to acknowledge that men face the pressures of body image just as acutely as women, and that we suffer from the harmful perpetuation of a single stereotype of the perfect, hairless, ab-riddled body with no discernible fat and those V-lines that haunt me in my sleep. It's where I learned that it's OK to lust after that stereotype as long as it doesn't rest in your mind as the only desirable version of manhood. That fat bodies are desirable, too. That chubby Chris Pratt is just as fuckable as ripped Chris Pratt, and probably more so.

I still have accepting to do. But I can finally say I'm happy being fat. Do I still ogle muscled men? Yes. Do I still have pictures of them pasted to my apartment walls? Yes. Do I know now that a desire for those bodies is not exclusive of my own desirability? Of course. And do I wish I could still fit under the bed? Well, sure. But only because I'm pretty sure I dropped a Twix down there, and I'd really like to find it.

RULES FOR A TOTALLY HEALTHY AND NOT-AT-ALL-MEDICALLY-CONCERNING LIFESTYLE

I am, by many accounts, a vision of absolute health. I eat no less than seven meals a day, so I'm constantly bursting with nutrition. I exercised for a whole hour once last year. And I chug a few bottles of wine throughout the week, which is basically the same as juicing, but with even more antioxidants. In fact, my doctor says the wine "probably won't kill you anytime soon," which is the closest thing to a medical endorsement I'm getting for my budding alcoholism, and I'll take it. Alas, nobody's offered to put me on the cover of *Men's Health*, or even the cover of a high-fiber cereal box with a gold medal around my neck, so I'm forced to cement my status as a health icon in my own way.

Here, a list of my tips for maintaining a strong, healthy, and not-at-all-medically-concerning lifestyle:

1. Any dessert with fewer calories than ice cream doesn't actually count as dessert and can be consumed with utter and complete abandon. FroYo is basically water, and can be drunk as such.

2. Chewy chocolate chip cookies are like celery: you burn off more calories than they're worth just from the energy you expend by eating them. Truly the only miracle food.

3. A single waffle with butter and syrup is the most well-balanced and nutritious meal on earth.

4. Eating a salad before or after eating a piece of cake cancels out the cake. Really, if you eat a salad, you can follow it with literally anything and it's nutritious. And if you slip in your diet and have too much to eat: follow it with salad and your stomach resets. That's just nutritional science.

5. Anything that's been dropped on the floor is good enough to eat, and anybody who tells you otherwise is weak.

6. Legally, they can't stop you from bringing chocolate lava cake into the gym.

7. Chewing is the body's way of trying to stop you from swallowing at the speed you really want.

8. Two pots of coffee a day is a perfectly acceptable way to sustain yourself with enough energy to watch TV without moving.

9. Eating a whole cake is the same as eating just one

piece, as long as you do it in the same amount of time.

10. Anything you eat as part of a contest doesn't count as eating. That's a hobby.

11. Chocolate milk is God's kale smoothie.

12. Bread is like a pillow for your stomach: essential for a good night's sleep.

13. Opening the refrigerator door counts as exercise.

14. Calories don't count if you can't see them, which is why you should always cover your food in a thick layer of ranch dressing.

15. A bowl of cereal every evening is essential to a good night's rest, except for Cheerios, which barely count as cereal and are an affront to the entire breakfast community.

16. If you're gonna eat an entire package of cookies, it's best to do it in one sitting so it still technically counts as one serving.

17. Putting honey in any drink makes it better for you.

18. If you're gonna drink a glass of wine, you might as well drink the whole bottle.

19. Tea from a cup with a saucer underneath always tastes better than tea with no saucer.

20. A side muffin has the same nutritional benefits as a side salad. It's on the side, so it doesn't count.

21. A nap is the best way to burn off calories because calories are always running around in their sleep.

ON MY OLD AND FRAGILE BODY, OR I FEEL BAD ABOUT MY EVERYTHING

Like most chubby gay nerds in Middle America, I was picked last in gym class every single time getting picked last was an option. Honestly, it would have been easier if my P.E. teachers had just announced it outright: "Captains, pick your teammates. And remember, the tubby red one in the glasses gets picked last." But that would have been too gracious, and a part of me thinks that gym teachers derive great pleasure from watching nature take its predetermined course, like in *National Geographic*, but instead of an elderly rhinoceros getting left by its herd to die in a river, it's a fat kid with a limp wrist getting shunted to the outfield.

Unsurprisingly, gym class was never fun for me or my body. I was big in all the wrong places, my limbs too thick and fleshy to properly coordinate with my brain. The bottoms of my legs were as stubby as my calves. My torso was just wide enough to ensure any foul ball always had an unmissable, plump target. And my big clunky feet moved just slow enough to make certain I'd never evade a direct, violent hit to the face. I was a living embodiment of Newton's little known Fourth Rule of Motion: "Every kickball in a state of brutal velocity continues in a state of brutal velocity until it applies itself to a gay nerd's brand-new Ray-Ban eyeglasses." I'm happy, at the very least, to have done my part for science.

My body always seemed just out of whack with my brain. When I ran—which I did sparingly, usually in the direction of an ice-cream-truck jingle—I never knew what to do with my arms, so they'd dangle uselessly next to my torso like an ostrich's scrawny wings, flailing in the wind. I had poor balance, and tipped over easily. And my limbs seemed to grow at a pace that apparently my body hadn't prepared for.

I went to the doctor to complain about muscle cramps and aches, in secret hope that he would absolve me from physical activity for the rest of time. Dr. Keith was his name, and he was himself an overly tall, gangly, and balding man. I'd hoped he would take pity on me as a fellow victim of his own body's apparent desire to outgrow itself. But no. "Growing pains," he told me. "Perfectly normal for a boy your age whose body is getting bigger."

I was ten years old, so I probably just said, "OK, thank you for your counsel, elderly sir." But I should've said it was fucking bullshit, because that's what growing pains are. Pain is supposed to be the body's way of telling your brain there's a problem. But what exactly was the problem? My body was . . .

what? Growing too fast? Growing too big? Growing at all? I never really got an answer.

He did tell me I was flat-footed, which apparently contributed to the aches in my legs and hips. But that's just more bullshit. Since when are feet too lazy to be in the shape of feet? What hope does the rest of my body have if the things it depends on to stand can't even do their job properly?

Growing pains and flat feet aside, my brain and my body still found ways to conspire against one another.

. . .

One summer day, in 1995, my aunt Bonnie set up a slip 'n' slide in her backyard, the kind of water slide that lies flat on the lawn and relies on running water and sheer force of will to propel whoever jumps on it from one end to the other. Of course, ours was not a real Slip 'N Slide. My family was much too cheap to invest in store-bought anything, much less store-bought water slides, like the one from Toys"R"Us with the multiracial children on the box, laughing heartily while gliding along their soft, slippery, inflatable Aquatic Wonderland. Instead, my aunt set down two large blue tarps on the hard ground, like we were preparing for heavy construction. She positioned the garden hose on one end, turned it on high to build up a current, and covered it in bath bubble soap for lubrication. Not unexpectedly, soap proved to be ineffective at turning a literal sheet of plastic into a slip 'n' slide, so she brought out the next logical option, a canister of pure vegetable oil, and covered the tarp in a thin, shiny layer, like a glistening leaf of lettuce.

I stood back and watched as my cousins, one by one, slid onto the tarp tummy-first and skidded along its surface like greasy chicken cutlets. I was the fattest and least athletic of the family, well known as the one most likely to end up hospitalized for skipping the wrong way. And so, I stood there and watched the others before trying it for myself.

When I'd finally worked up the courage, I took a running start (or as much of a running start as my bulky legs allowed), leapt as high as my flat feet would take me, and crossed my legs midair like I was sitting down for story time. Why my brain thought this was a logical pose to strike is beyond me. I think I envisioned gliding along the tarp butt-first, and sliding to the end with my hands resting adorably beneath my chin like I was posing for a glamour shot. Perhaps a part of me wanted to take the moment to show off, to use this dumb garbage water slide to show everybody that I could do what they were doing, and then some! Fuck you for always thinking I was the dumpy unathletic family nerd. I can read books and hit this slip 'n' slide like a champion.

What happened instead was far from glamorous. The tip of my tailbone came down on the hard ground with a heavy thunk, and every ounce of air in my lungs escaped in one thick howl. I slid lifelessly to the end of the tarp, and lay there motionless. My cousins formed a circle around my limp, ungainly body, not breathing, my eyes staring up at nothing in the sky, while my aunt rushed to blow air in my face. I started breathing eventually. Nothing was broken. I was just an idiot who jumped tailbone-first onto a patch of solid earth. "Why would you do that?" my aunt screamed at me. "What were you thinking?" But I didn't have an answer. My brain just had it in for my body, I guess.

Indeed, not even a year later, I started climbing a small bush—a bush! a piece of shrubbery!—during an innocuous game of tag, immediately fell backwards, and broke my left elbow in two. Some say I was pushed. But that's only because they were trying to find a logical explanation where there wasn't one. My body didn't follow the rules of logic, after all. The doctors said I'd need pins in my arm, and frankly, I welcomed them. Anything that replaced my body with machinery seemed like a good idea when my actual flesh was doing nothing besides getting itself into constant trouble.

A few years later, on the very first day of summer vacation, I was riding a scooter—not a motor scooter, mind you, just a run-of-the-mill, push-it-with-your-flat-foot scooter—and my brain decided it was a good idea to throw the Frisbee mid-glide. So I threw it, immediately tossed myself off balance, tried stopping my fall with a folded fist, and landed on my wrist. I felt my arm crunch beneath my weight.

"It's not broken," my cousin assured me. "I've seen a lot of broken bones, and you're fine." Never mind that my forearm flopped like jelly when I tried to fix my glasses. But it turned out my cousin was right, in a way. It wasn't broken, at least not all the way through, and a doctor spent an hour shooting me with numbing agents and twisting the bone until it broke cleanly. "It'll heal better this way," he said between twists. But I knew I'd be back again, if not for this, then for something else.

In fact, I spent almost every summer in various stages of recovery from one recently incurred injury or another. One summer, I stepped on a piece of glass and sliced open the heel of my foot. Another summer, I stepped on a beehive. Another summer still, I stepped off a curb and somehow sprained my wrist.

My body would always find a way to betray me.

Meanwhile, despite my body's resistance, gym class continued on, growing more complicated and militaristic. Just when I thought I'd mastered the art of evading the kickball, we'd graduate to dodgeball—the most cruel and unusual way to teach children jihadi warfare—and I'd have to learn a whole new set of elusion tactics. Once my wounds healed from dodgeball, we'd level up to basketball (hardened leather is much less forgiving on the flesh), then football (hardened leather, now pointy!), then volleyball (softer ball, way more flailing limbs), then badminton (sports, now with metal weapons!), then tennis (metal weapons, but heavier!), and so on and so forth until I could identify the type of ball walloping me in the face with my eyes closed and my hands tied behind my back.

By the time we moved on to track and field, I was in high school, and physical activity became less about breaking the human body, and more about all-out destroying the human spirit. We were introduced to the "pacer test," a medieval-torture-device-turned-physical-contest in which an audiotape projected a series of ever-quickening beeps as we students were forced to sprint from one side of the gym to the other before the tape chimed next. The number of times you could sprint back and forth without failing to beat the buzzer or succumbing to death was translated into a value applied to your worth in life. And not to brag, but my value clocked in at around three whole times, which statistically meant I was faster than a country turkey, but slower than an angry hippopotamus. I'm not even ashamed to say I ran a twenty-one-minute mile in ninth grade, and to this day it remains the fastest I've ever moved.

Perhaps gym was simply the educational system's way of pushing both our bodies and minds to new extremes. Perhaps that's why my body has always been so aggressively frail, because I never tried hard enough to make it stronger. But I always preferred to treat my body like a set of fine china: too fancy and delicate to use (unless the pope is in town).

It's no surprise, then, that I've grown distrustful of physical activity in my mature state. For me, fitness will always equal shame and pain, broken bones and the bad kind of balls to the face. Going to the gym will always feel off, because I'll never feel like I belong. The people who are there are the people who were picked before me, the people whose bodies actually work, the people whose bones are strong and intact.

Or at least that's what I told myself when I canceled my gym membership and the woman on the phone told me I was making a terrible mistake. Maybe one day, Sheri from LA Fitness will read this chapter and understand that she saved herself a lawsuit. You hear that, Sheri? YOU TRIED TO SHAME ME FOR NOT JOINING YOUR FUCKING GYM, BUT I PROBABLY WOULD'VE DIED THERE.

You're welcome, Sheri. And you're welcome, body.

ON NEAR-DEATH EXPERIENCES, OR THAT TIME I CHOKED ON A TAQUITO

Braces are an abomination. I know this is an obvious observation to most people, but I had braces for six painful, raw-gummed, swollen-tongued years, so I feel particularly entitled to complain about this one, and I'd like anybody who never suffered, or who didn't suffer as awfully as I did, to understand the agony I endured for more than half a decade. Because six years is an abnormally long time to have braces, especially when the entire journey fucked up my relationship with food forever. But let's start at the beginning.

Braces are barbaric. They are the only means of medieval torture that have carried over into common application today, presumably because they keep teenagers from giving enjoyable blow jobs until they're at least eighteen. (Which has less to do with the fact that your teeth feel like knives and more to do with the fact that, whenever you smile or speak, you look like the Terminator registering his next mortal enemy.) You'd think, surely, that dental science and engineering would have, since biblical times, advanced beyond installing an entire airplane hangar worth of sheet metal inside a child's mouth. But you'd be wrong. If anything, the dental profession has regressed even further, and I'm predicting that full-body metal braces that tie around the back of your scalp will be making a comeback in the next five years.

(Actually, I don't even know if kids still get braces these days, or if everybody has those invisible braces that go right over your teeth, or if robots just replace your teeth with better teeth while you sleep. But in my day, we had metal-as-fuck braces, and they were the worst.)

The real problem, of course, is that braces all but destroy your ability to enjoy a decent meal. The entire dental industry is anti-food, and I'm sure there's some crack dentist somewhere who's gonna write me a letter and tell me that eating a healthy diet will make my teeth whiter or some shit, but you can save the ink, buddy, because the teeth I have left are perfectly fine without your meddling and I know you just want to stop me from eating delicious caramels. I remain convinced that they only make you answer one question when you want to be a dentist, and that question is: "Will you make people feel like absolute garbage for everything they eat?" And if you answer yes—congratulations, you're a dentist. It's like every time I ever go to the dentist, all he can talk about is every meal he finds in between my molars. He's always like, "Hey pal, looks like you missed a whole bunch of food in here while you were flossing." And I'm always like, "Joke's on you, friend. I've never flossed even once in my whole life."

But when I was little, my crack dentist wasn't happy enough telling me passive-aggressively to brush my teeth every six months, so he was all like, "I think you need braces." And then, presumably so I could mentally prepare my tubby body for the deprivation it was about to endure, he gave me a manual of all the things you weren't allowed to eat while you had braces, which included just about every food you can possibly imagine besides bananas that have been pre-chewed by a parent or legal guardian and regurgitated into your mouth.

I got braces in the fifth grade, on one of those glorious days in elementary school when we were catered some local delicacy, like McDonald's or the knockoff Subway or pizza from the place inside the bowling alley. Our school brought in these hot lunches every month, I assume, as a way to keep us from rioting, and they were my favorite days of the year. I kept a calendar for the sole purpose of tracking hot-lunch days.

By some cruel twist of fate, the day I got braces coincided with fried-chicken day, and the moment I bit into that crispy chicken breast with my newly metallic teeth was like biting into a stick of dynamite that had been dipped in burning acid and wrapped in angry bees. My entire mouth exploded in pain, because apparently, when you get braces, your teeth and gums freak out about how everything is changing and nothing will ever be the same, and decide to set themselves on fire the second you try to use them for their intended purpose. Defeated, I set aside the chicken and tried my luck with a biscuit, but my teeth were like, "Nice try, asshole, but you might as well get used to never eating delicious baked breads ever again," and then I tried the mashed potatoes and gravy, but even *they* proved too painful to swish around. So I vowed to jump in front of the school bus the next morning and end it all for good.

Except I didn't, because I was far too scared of moving vehicles and also our bus driver, so I just persisted in agony for the next six years with a mouth full of metal that made eating the most difficult thing in the world.

But here's the thing. Braces weren't even the worst part of having braces. The worst part was all the preparation required for getting braces, because apparently you can't just slap those babies in and call it a day, you have to get your mouth ready with a whole host of awful procedures that exist for the sole purpose of creating moments that will scar you well into adulthood and make you, once again, fear food entirely.

The first thing they do when they assess you for braces is a thing dentists called impressions. Impressions are a process in which the dentist fills a tiny round metal tray with a glob of clay putty he scooped from the bottom of an abandoned marsh, and smashes it against the roof of your mouth to get a 3-D rendering of your teeth. To make it worse, the dentist people try to flavor the putty to taste like bubble gum, but really, it tastes like it was made by an alien who has never tasted bubble gum before, which is to say, it tastes like the inside of a recently douched anus. Inevitably, the dentist will overfill the putty tray, which means, while he presses it against the roof of your mouth, half of the stuff goes down your throat and tickles that part of your tonsils that I like to call the Violent Vomit Button.

This may go without saying, but the action of someone jamming an entire handful of ass putty into your mouth is officially the most gag-inducing thing you can do to another human, and yes, I'm including whatever it is you're thinking about right now. It smelled like burning flesh and tasted like intestines, and it was being used as a weapon of war that attacked as many of my senses at once as possible. So yes, I threw up. Well, actually, I gagged a lot at first, like that real deep gag you do sometimes that sounds like a sea lion calling for its mother. And *then* I threw up a lot. It didn't matter how many times they screamed, "JUST CLOSE YOUR EYES AND RELAX YOUR THROAT, YOUR MASCARA IS RUNNING," I puked all over that dentist and his dumb tray of butt clay and not at all into the bucket they were holding under my face to catch the barf. And you know what? They did that shit *three times*, until my gags yielded only dry heaves, because apparently throwing up all over the little clay version of your mouth makes it unusable and they have to do it until there isn't any vomit in all the little teeth holes.

(Side note: I heard that dentist call one of his assistants a bitch one time, so I have zero regrets about vomiting all over that bastard. If I could, I'd go back and vomit on him again, because my stomach is bigger now and can hold even more vomit.)

And the worst part is, those fucking impressions screwed me over, 'cause they sent them to the lab or whatever weird sex palace they send children's mouth molds to, and they came back and they were like, "Guess what? Not only are your teeth not straight, your mouth is too small, like some kind of idiot." And they were telling the truth. My mouth was, in medical terms, narrower than a pigeon's beak. Or at least that's how the doctors described it. Apparently, my mouth was too narrow to fit all my teeth, because the two in the front started kinda growing into one another, like two awkward kids at a crowded party getting smashed together by a bunch of people dancing to "Mambo No. 5." It's a relatively common malady, which, if left untreated, guaranteed that I would grow up to be either a very successful prostitute, or one of those guys who auditions for television talent shows with the ability to whistle entire Mozart compositions through his nose. Coupled with a mild case of sleep apnea, it meant that my throat was basically the anatomical equivalent of a collapsed Chilean coal mine. (Thirty-three men had been briefly lost in it.)

The only solution to this condition was to install a janky contraption the doctors called an "expander," conceived by the same sadists who designed mattresses in the nineties or the wooden benches at Starbucks or any number of other bullshit things created solely to bring nothing but torment and pain to everyone, particularly narrow-mouthed children like myself. Here's how it worked: The expander was a metal apparatus that the dentist literally installed in the top of my mouth with actual cement, which I'm pretty sure he was not even legally allowed to use, because he was a dentist and not a fucking construction worker, but that's not the point here. He cemented that thing to my mouth, and then gave my mother a tiny key, and whispered in her ear instructions for how to use it. Every night, just before bed, she was to insert the key into my gaping mouth, slide it into a teeny hole on the bottom of the device, and turn it three times, and with every turn, the spacer would crank wider, like those torture devices they used in the Middle Ages to rip people apart, except instead of ripping someone apart, it would slowly lurch the roof of my mouth wider and wider. My mother claimed it was just as painful for her to crank the key, because she knew how much it hurt and a mother feels the pain of her children or some shit like that, but that's bull, because it felt like a very tiny person with a very tiny chainsaw had climbed inside of my head and started to chop off my face from within, and I'm pretty sure she didn't fucking feel that. In fact, I would go so far as to say that she even enjoyed it some nights, because I was a smart-ass, and my narrow mouth and I deserved every bit of pain we had coming to us.

In addition to the physical pain, though, the device was a general pain in the ass to live with. It was a giant hunk of steel cemented to the top of my mouth, which you'd think would be a perfectly discreet place to keep a hunk of steel, but turns out, not so much. For one, metal of the medical variety is always somehow sharper and more jagged than the metal they use for, say, barbed wire or hacksaws. So I spent most of the four months I wore this device hoping that I wouldn't wake up one morning to find half of my tongue lying next to me in bed. It also turns out that your tongue generally needs the full space of your mouth in order to speak in a language that other humans understand, so I sounded like I was constantly trying to get an oversized bite of peanut-butter-and-jelly sandwich unstuck from the back of my teeth.

And worst of all, it was virtually impossible to eat anything even closely resembling solid food the entire time that thing was up there. My only means of nourishment was to rip all of my food into tiny pieces, delicately put them on my tongue like I was feeding a hummingbird, and swish them slowly around my mouth until they were melty enough to swallow. If I took too big of a bite, or swished too quickly, the food would somehow find its way up *into* the expander, and lodge itself in the tiny space between the metal and the roof of my mouth. And then I'd have to spend hours trying to effectively suck my own mouth to get the food unstuck, or somehow jam a knife in the tiny space in the front of the thing to push the food out the tiny space in the back. It was, as they say, a disaster waiting to happen.

And disaster struck, as these things always tend to do, during my brother's surprise sixteenth birthday party. Perhaps, subconsciously, I simply could not stand to attend an event at which I was not the sole center of attention. Or perhaps, on some deeper level, this milestone reminded me of my own mortality and my body decided to simply end it all before it had the chance to get any worse. But more than likely, disaster struck because we had made the mistake of combining a high-pressure social gathering with steaming-hot appetizers and a minor orthodontic surgical device.

Here's what happened.

I didn't particularly like parties as a kid, especially when they weren't for me, and especially when they were surprise parties I wasn't told about because I couldn't be trusted to keep a secret. If I'd had my way, I would've spent the evening in my bedroom, playing with my Pokémon cards in peace, descending only to retrieve a slice of ice cream cake, which I would've dragged back to my room to swish slowly in my mouth piece by tiny piece. Parties always felt like too much effort, mostly because I was ten, and didn't have the stamina to sustain more than three minutes of small talk. You know what everybody asks you when you're ten? "How is school going?" How the fuck do you think school is going? I'm in the fifth grade. I colored a map today, and some kid swallowed an eraser. I don't have time to be answering this garbage.

But of course, my mother forced me to attend because that's the only way she would give me cake, and I had no choice but to make conversation, or whatever conversation I could muster with a chunk of metal dentistry filling most of my throat.

And herein lay the problem. You put a child who doesn't want to be at a party at a party and surround him with people he doesn't want to talk to, and he does the only thing that ten-year-olds know how to do with any sort of confidence: he eats. He eats whatever you put in front of him. Anything at all that keeps him from having to speak, or emote, or interact socially with any human besides someone who may be standing in the way of food.

Now, we never really had appetizers at parties. We were more of a chip-and-dip family. If you came to a party hungry, well, that was your own damn fault, 'cause all that we promised in the invitation was cake and maybe a single box of wine. The day of any party was usually rife with cleaning and dusting and screaming, and my parents rarely had time to do all three of those things, let alone time to prepare pigs in a blanket.

But today was a special occasion (i.e., my mother had made it to Sam's Club with enough time to buy a cake and a few boxes of frozen finger foods), and we had a hopping spread of sliders, barbecue chicken wings, and taquitos. And my tubby self couldn't get enough of it.

First of all, it was food, and food meant I didn't have to talk to anybody. But more important, it was appetizers, which are inarguably, categorically better than regular-sized food. It's like Jesus said, "Take the same amount of flavor as a full-sized adult food, but put it into the body of this tiny baby food, and also roll it into a stick, because everything is obviously better in phallic form, and BAM, you got yourself the greatest food-stuff in the world." I mean, I was only a kid, and I couldn't know this at the time, but I would make the argument now that fried mac 'n' cheese balls fresh from the oven, no matter how sloppily they are made, are greater than the best sex you can possibly imagine in your entire life. (The thought of combining these two things is too much for my brain to even comprehend.)

So let's recap. I was an awkward, chubby kid, standing at a party I didn't want to be at, with a mouth full of metal that tasted like a handful of quarters, next to a plate of the greatest food created by Jesus himself, a food we did not get to eat but once every five to ten years. My brain said, "You know this isn't going to end well. Just wait for your ice cream cake, and everything will be fine." But my stomach said, "Eat the taquitos, tubby. We're not gonna live forever." And you sure as hell know which one I listened to.

I took the biggest taquito on the tray, dipped it as far into the bowl of sour cream as it would go, and inhaled that thing like I was a congressman who had just burned down an orphanage to make room for an oil rig and was sucking eagerly on the end of a cigar. But here was the problem. I quite literally inhaled it. Like, for some reason, I actually sucked on the sour-creamed end of the taquito, presumably to extract as much flavor as I could and prolong this savory bliss. But the dried, frozen meat inside the rolled shell somehow came loose and shot to the back of my throat, and when I coughed, the meat came back up just enough for half of it to catch in the metal expander and lodge there, the other half dangling down the back of my throat.

So there I was, in the center of my brother's surprise sixteenth birthday party, involuntarily deep-throating the dried beefy center of a taquito, and freaking the fuck out. If you've ever seen footage of a pelican swallowing a fish that somehow swims back up its gullet, that's exactly what was happening to me, except it wasn't a fish, it was a hard rod of spicy meat, and it wasn't swimming out of me so much as it was being held immovably halfway between a swallow and a regurgitation.

I panicked. I looked around and nobody seemed to notice I was being slowly choked to death by the meat of a taquito colluding with the metal brace on the roof of my mouth. I started coughing, and then waving, and then fearfully grabbing my neck, and if I hadn't been so afraid I was experiencing the end, I would've enjoyed the melodrama of it all, but something about dying via taquito didn't feel quite dramatic enough to accept—I'd prefer to die in a blaze set by Beyoncé's own hands—so I fought. And by fought, I mean I ran in panic to my mother, who opened my mouth like she did when the dog snatches a dropped piece of chocolate, reached into my esophagus, and ripped the meat free.

I took a deep breath of oxygen and probably fainted, for maximum dramatic effect. And even though I spent the rest of the party as the focus of everyone's empathy, I could not forgive the hunk of metal in my mouth for turning food against me.

So here is my message, which I give to you as the survivor of this unspeakable trauma: Do not trust dentists. Do not trust orthodontists. Do not trust anybody who dares insert into your mouth a tiny tray of butthole putty, or a steel torture device, or a string of jagged metal braces. They are designed to turn you against the only thing you will ever love. And if you let them, they will succeed.

A BRIEF LIST
OF THINGS THAT
I DON'T KNOW

1. I have never once successfully folded any type of bed linen, fitted or otherwise, which is why I tend to avoid washing my sheets altogether, and also why my bedroom constantly smells like someone just microwaved a bag of popcorn.

2. I don't know what a retirement plan is. I don't know what 401(k) means or why the k is always hiding in those parentheses. I don't know what "escrow" is, or if that has anything to do with retirement, but I feel like it does because adults are always using these words together. I don't know what a certified public accountant is supposed to do besides wear short-sleeve button-downs and wire-rimmed glasses. I don't know anything about the national debt. And I don't get why so many elderly people in Florida are allowed to vote.

3. I order food for delivery every single day of the week, sometimes twice in one day if it's a special

occasion, like Thanksgiving or a Saturday, and more often than not, it's only because I want a slice of chocolate fudge layer cake and I have to pretend like I'm ordering a full meal around it and not just paying for someone to bring me a single container of frosted sugar.

4. I don't think I could keep a baby alive by myself for more than maybe forty minutes, mostly because I know you're supposed to rock babies back and forth, but I don't know how hard to rock them before the rocking would be considered violent shaking and I know that's how Lenny killed that woman in the book about the rabbits.

5. I've only really cleaned my bathroom once in the last year, mostly because I don't know how often you're supposed to clean a bathroom, since once a week seems like too often, and so does once every two weeks. By the third week it's too disgusting to even look at, and if I tried to clean it, I'd probably just throw up and make it all worse anyway, so might as well just wait until I move out or the entire apartment building burns down.

6. I don't know how to butter toast without ripping a ragged hole through the center of the slice every single time, and then all I have for breakfast is a hot piece of bread with a giant butter hole in the middle, which is generally why I avoid attempting to prepare food for myself at all costs.

7. I'm terrible at gift-giving, which is sort of a test of how good you are at being a competent adult

sufficient in sustaining relationships with other competent adults. I mean, even cats give gifts, even though their gifts are usually mouse carcasses, but at least they put some thought into it. The best I can do is an Applebee's gift card I bought at CVS.

8. I'm fairly certain that there's a dead mouse behind my bed, but I'm too afraid to move my mattress and confirm it, because as long as it's not confirmed there's at least a possibility that there isn't a dead mouse lying inches away from my face while I sleep.

9. I'm self-destructive, but not in the dramatic way that drug addicts on *CSI* are. Like, I've never snorted cocaine off a stripper's dick before, or any other body part for that matter. But I'm still slowly destroying myself. I routinely finish an entire box of soft-baked chocolate chip cookies in one sitting, and I haven't exercised since one of the Bushes was president.

10. I don't know what my bra size is.

ON MICHIGAN

My family was never a Disneyland family.

I always resented my classmates who belonged to Disney-land families, the haughty children who walked into class halfway through October and announced that they'd be missing school for an entire week while they gallivanted down to Florida to visit Cinderella and her whore sisters. "Have fun catching syphilis from Mickey Mouse," I'd sneer under my breath, or at least that's what I *would* have sneered if I'd known what syphilis was back then. To make it worse, those kids would always come back with Mickey Mouse–shaped water bottles and a week's worth of gaudy themed T-shirts, just to remind everybody that going to Disneyland was not a one-time luxury, but a permanent promotion in status, lest anybody should forget.

My parents always gave my brother and me a litany of excuses as to why we'd never go to Disneyland, chief among them being that my mother refused to get on an airplane (and driving together for anything longer than a couple of hours at most was out of the question). I always found this excuse insufficient, considering that my mother had flown on airplanes before—twice, in fact—most recently to Hawaii, some twenty years earlier on her and my father's honeymoon, and before then, as a haughty child herself, to none other than Disneyland. Perhaps she'd caught syphilis from Mickey Mouse, I thought. But more than likely she was simply a hypocrite.

The real excuse, or at least the one that was supposed to keep us from rioting, was that our very own Disneyland—basically just as good, but without all those pesky lines and stifling crowds and uninhibited fun—was just a two-hour drive away in sunny, breezy, coastal southern Michigan, home of the crumbling American auto industry and boundless amusement for children of all ages.

When you live in "the greater Chicagoland area"—a bullshit name for those parts of Indiana, Wisconsin, and suburban Illinois that have absolutely no right referring to themselves as Chicago but need some semblance of an identity to cling to, God bless them—you are fed a constant onslaught of commercials on television advertising the majestic forested hills of Michigan as the one true vacation destination. This is, of course, entirely absurd. Not to shit on Michigan, but there are far better vacation spots in the Midwest alone. And sure, Michigan's got gurgling brooks and crisp lakes full of fish bigger than grown men and miles upon miles of fresh forests, or some garbage like that. But Wisconsin's got the Wisconsin Dells, the water-park capital of the world, according to the brochure, and no child wants to hang out around a babbling river—unless you're a character in *Bridge to Terabithia* and you wanna die—especially not when that babbling river is one state away from the largest indoor water park in the United States.

But my uncle's family owned a cottage in Michigan, a small house on a tiny lake about fifteen miles inland from Lake Michigan proper. And apart from the month's worth of supplies my mother insisted on purchasing for a week of vacation, going to Michigan was basically free, at least compared to Disneyland. And so, every summer, instead of contracting ringworm in a communal men's shower somewhere in the bowels of Wisconsin like a normal midwestern family, we'd pile into a sedan—my mom, dad, brother, and me, along with the dog and our turtle, Cornpop, who traveled in a damp bucket between my brother's legs—and drove two hours to the town of Sister Lakes, where the paradise of small-town Michigan awaited.

Two hours traveling now is a virtual cakewalk, but back then, a two-hour drive in the backseat of a cramped car was my own personal hell, not only because of my family's less-than-pleasant digestive failings, but also because of my mother's unrelenting need to pack an entire deli's worth of groceries into every available space. Half of those drives, I had boxes of granola bars and packaged pastries pooling at my feet. I rested my head on open bundles of blueberry muffins and twisted bags of hamburger buns, stacked atop a giant cooler that sat between my brother and me in the backseat. In my lap, if I wasn't charged with holding the dog, who threw up on cue at least every fifteen minutes, I'd be forced to hold some other item we couldn't have traveled without, like a case of beer or box of wine. Mobility was limited, at best.

To get to Sister Lakes, Michigan, from Chicago, there was

approximately ten minutes of suburbia, followed by an hour of open highway, followed by fifty minutes of pure, concentrated countryside, which is to say, absolutely fucking nothing. I'd spend what felt like hours staring at the back of my mother's seat in front of me, shifting slightly, as much as I could, beneath the weight of whatever box of meats was crushing my thighs.

"Look at the cows!" my mother would shout every twenty minutes, and if we turned immediately and glared out the part of the window uninhibited by stacks of frozen waffles and sliced bread, we'd catch just a blurry, passing glimpse of a pasture that quickly gave way to cornstalks or blueberry bushes or whatever boring crop infests those parts of America that most of us try not to think about.

I'd always know we were getting close to the cottage when signs of modern society began to vanish, when stoplights at intersections started giving way to rickety stop signs hanging from strings over dusty roads, and gas-station pumps started looking less like gas-station pumps and more like butter-churning barrels.

The cottage itself was at the end of a winding gravel road hidden by a dense thicket of trees and brush, and was nearly impossible to see, even in broad daylight. If ever I managed to fall asleep, I'd be jerked awake by the rattle of the car lurching along the rocky street, shaking the towers of food around my face and sending one box or another tumbling to the floor. The dog would barf one last time and finally we'd be there.

Of course, this should be obvious, but if a lake is surrounded by overgrown, almost impassable vegetation—so dense that only a gravel road suffices as an acceptable throughway—maybe it shouldn't be colonized by tourists. There was another house along the gravel road, inhabited by lake-town natives, who I assumed had been driven insane by years spent gestating in relative obscurity. Whenever we'd drive past, without fail there was always a child in one of the windows brandishing a rifle.

Welcome to Disneyland.

The cottage was a relic of the 1970s, a modest-sized structure with all the trappings you'd expect of an old lake house: musty carpet, wood-paneled walls full of kitschy wooden ducks, and wrought-iron birds alongside framed photos of aunts and uncles and cousins holding up fish caught twenty years before. The house had the perpetual whiff of dampness, the smell of decades of wet feet walking on wooden floors, sunblock and sweat dripped onto carpet, the accumulation of dust and dirt and cobwebs settled permanently in those nine off-summer months when a vacation home goes unoccupied. It would have been a comforting smell, if not for the year someone found a dead squirrel in the closet, in the center of an old, rolled-up rug. I hesitate to think how long it was there, whether the fresh country air we had been breathing year after year was actually just airborne squirrel decay.

At least fifteen of my family members would go to the cottage at once—my grandparents, my mother and her three sisters, their husbands, all five of my cousins and me, plus the dogs and the turtle and anything else that managed to fit inside the trunk of the car. Each family unit would cram into one of the four bedrooms, which means I'd get stuck on a deflated air mattress on the floor beside my parents' bed, my brother on a cot at the end of the bed, an arrangement that virtually guaranteed all of us would go an entire week without sleep.

Every night, I'd fall asleep, and in a matter of minutes, my brother would whip a pillow forcefully at my face to stop me from snoring. (My oversized tonsils made any attempts to curb my snoring nearly impossible.) Pissed, I'd groggily whip the pillow back, but given my homosexual aim, a lamp would fall over, the dog would start barking, my dad would start grumbling, my mom would start shouting, and before long, the entire house would be listening to us screaming at one another to go to sleep.

Conflict never contained itself just to our bedroom, though. Virtually every year, by the end of the week, everyone was pissed at someone else, for one reason or another. You put fifteen people in a small house in the August heat, with a cooler of alcohol per adult, there's bound to be some drama. After all, once the sun sets in the middle of nowhere, there isn't much to do besides drink. This is how reality television is made, after all. At the worst of it, in the midst of an after-dinner board game sometime in 2000, some innocuous disagreement over the rules led my grandmother to throw her arms in the air and shout, "That's it! We're out of here!" And she promptly made my grandfather pack all their belongings in the trunk and drive back to Chicago in the middle of the night, never to return to the cottage again.

To complete the idyllic vacation ambience, the cottage plumbing was as archaic as the structure itself, and to stave off the literal shit show that fifteen people taking daily showers and bowel movements could wreak on the system, we enforced a strict "if it's yellow, let it mellow" policy in regards to toilet flushing, giving the hallways an added air of dank stench. But, inevitably, the pumps would give way, and the grass in the back of the house would start bubbling up with thick sewage. To make it all worse, my uncle's parents—the cottage owners—installed a toilet in the corner of the large room we used as a pantry, which, on the one hand, alleviated stress on the otherwise lone toilet upstairs, but, on the other hand, added a layer of filth to our snacks, which we kept on a table on the other side of the room, even after the toilet was consecrated. It was all, to say the very least, a less than ideal living arrangement, to be sardined into a decaying house, floating on a river of shit, delirious for lack of sleep.

Of course, the real draw of Michigan—what they talked about in those horrible commercials—was not to be confined indoors, but to experience the bounty of nature, or some bullshit like that. The cottage was simply the backdrop, a place to sleep (or not) so you'd be rested the next morning for another day spent entirely outdoors, away from television, the Internet, and the refrigerator.

The lake the cottage was on was quite beautiful, if you're into that sort of thing. In the morning, when the sky was clear, the water still, the sun at a manageable angle, I could almost understand why businessmen faked their own deaths to escape their families for a place like this. But the beauty lasted only as long as you kept your distance. The water itself was nearly opaque with clouds of sand upset by whatever marine life dwelled at its depths. If you tossed a rock into the water, it took only a few inches before it all but disappeared, eaten by a brown fog. Over the years, we saw all manner of oversized fish, snakes, and snapping turtles, some the size of kickballs, emerging from the deep, and that was only what we spotted from the surface, through the seaweed. It amazes me still that we swam regularly in that water. One year, I found a tick crawling on the nape of my neck while I was drying off beside the lake, and spent the rest of our vacation convinced that I'd contracted Lyme disease. Even now, when I think about the fact that I was once willingly submerged in that water, it gives me that uncomfortable tingly feeling at the base of my spine. But then again, that might just be the Lyme disease.

· · ·

It amazes me most that we continued to visit this place, considering everything that went wrong there. Idyllic as it was—poop puddles and decaying squirrels aside—the cottage was site to some of the more physically traumatizing moments of my childhood. It was there that I broke my first bone, after all, falling backwards from a bush in the yard, snapping my elbow and leaving me in a cast for the rest of the summer.

And that was only the beginning.

One summer, while we were swimming in a part of the lake that wasn't yet overrun with floating branches or goopy seaweed, one of my cousins spotted a snake slithering along the grass near the water and shouted, "SNAAAAAKE!" We all scurried ashore, screaming all the way, not to escape it, but to run after it. None of us had ever caught a snake before. We'd seen everything else up close: giant fish, a soft-shelled turtle, an oversized toad. Our very own turtle, Cornpop, was a catch my brother had made years earlier, back when my parents were apparently foolish enough to let their children take wildlife home. (For the record, I'm pretty sure my mother assumed the turtle would die before she'd have to worry about it, but that motherfucker lived for almost twenty years, so take that, Debbie.) But a snake was exciting stuff. Uncharted territory.

Personally, I never understood the appeal of chasing after snakes, or any wildlife for that matter, because I've seen *Anaconda* and I know that all snakes, including the teeny ones, are capable of swallowing an entire human body and regurgitating the half-digested remains in an abandoned warehouse somewhere in the Amazon. Chasing after a snake seemed to be an easy way of asking for trouble. Even if we didn't catch him, he would go off and tell his snake friends that a band of children were harassing him, and before you know it, he'd be back with a mob, except this time, they'd be in my air mattress and my mouth would be open because of the tonsil thing and it's just a whole big nightmare. I wasn't one to take that sort of risk. The closest I'd ever been to a snake was Halloween when I was eleven years old, the year I dressed as Steve Irwin, the Crocodile Hunter, a costume that amounted to short khaki shorts, a matching V-neck button-up, and a stuffed toy snake wrapped around my arm. But even the stuffed snake made me uncomfortable, and not only because I tripped over it that night and put a snag in the skin-colored tights my mother insisted I wear beneath the khaki costume to protect me from the cold. A snake is a snake.

But when everybody is running after one, you get caught up in the adventure of it all, the Steve Irwin part of your brain takes over, and before you know it, you're chasing and screaming and whooping.

So I chased after that disgusting thing alongside everybody else, all of us barefoot, as it weaved in and out of the tall grass and under overturned paddleboats and through a pile of firewood, all the while out of our reach, until it finally went wriggling back into the water. We were city children, after all. No match for a country snake.

But amidst the excitement, amidst the running and screaming and whooping, my foot landed in a pile of dirt somewhere along the shore and I felt a stinging pain shoot up my leg. I let out a yelp and lifted my leg to see the bottom of my foot, thinking I'd stepped on a sharp rock or maybe a bit of broken glass, but what I saw instead was a bee taking his final breath, his stinger firmly in the bottom of my heel. I'd never been stung by a bee before, and it wasn't the best feeling in the world. But, like stepping on a used meth needle, it's really most alarming because you don't know what happens afterward.

I cursed the bee under my breath and brushed his corpse off my heel, and that's when I noticed the hole he'd crawled out of, in the middle of the pile of dirt upset by my feet, and the other holes around it, all teeming with other bees newly incensed by my presence.

It was their nest, I realized, and I'd crushed it with my thumping foot. I'd run right into their hive, I'd killed one of their brothers, and now they were angry.

Now, I should pause to point out that this is one of the many ways in which humanity is no match for nature: *there are fucking underground beehives.* As in, bees that live in the fucking ground. I'd also like to take this moment to formally accuse Winnie the Pooh of failing to prepare me for this phenomenon. Thanks to Winnie, I'd spent years going about life assuming delicious honey-producing beehives were found exclusively aboveground, and I fully blame him for my ignorance on this subject. But it took only a few moments for me to draw a few clear conclusions about underground beehives, or rather, one very important conclusion: underground beehives do not like getting stepped on. In fact, they very much dislike getting stepped on, so much so that when they *are* stepped on, they happen to overreact and, despite their trespasser's loud and fervent attempts at de-escalation, attack accordingly.

The bees rose up in unison and set about swarming not just me, but all of us children, in retaliation. Sure, I was the one who had destroyed their nest, but they attacked us all without asking questions. Our parents watched from afar as we all came screaming back to the house, bringing the swarm with us, wailing like mad as the cloud of bees chased after us. The bees stung and bit any exposed limb with impunity as we ran, our arms flailing, swinging whatever objects we could to knock out as many bees as possible at once. When we reached the house, everybody scrambled indoors, yelping at the final stings, swinging away the most committed soldiers.

Inside, the house became a full-blown triage unit, like the kind you see in movies about the Civil War, with soldiers lying in filthy beds, biting into chunks of wood while nurses saw off their exploded legs. All of us children collapsed onto the ground in various states of panic and pain, cries and screams piercing the air. It was utter madness.

I'm not proud to admit that I managed, somehow, to escape with only the single initial sting, while everybody else wailed in pain around me. Naturally, of course, I was the only one to have *stepped* on a bee, which is a lot like accidentally shooting off your foot with a rifle. But I couldn't let on that I'd caused this whole mess and made off with only a single wound, so I writhed alongside everybody else.

Still, I remain convinced that there were at least twelve other things to blame before me, including the snake, the cousin who spotted the snake, Winnie the Pooh, and most of all, the cottage itself, which I continue to believe is cursed.

. . .

The trips to Michigan continued year after year, my family's enthusiasm undisturbed by mass bee attacks, poop rivers, and ongoing feuds. And the curse showed no signs of relenting either.

Two summers after the bee attack, when our wounds finally showed signs of healing, I went to the cottage with my aunt, uncle, and cousins a night early. My parents and brother were driving up the next morning, but I begged and pleaded to hitch a ride the night before, reminding my mother that without me in the car, she could fill my seat with another twenty, maybe even thirty, dinners, plus any number of extra breads, fruit platters, wrapped pies, and brownie trays, and I just couldn't imagine us surviving the week with anything less. Of course, she relented, if only to get me to stop listing foods, and let me go.

I felt guilty that night, once we arrived, to have the entire bedroom to myself. I could sleep in the real bed instead of an air mattress, and snore as loud as I wanted without retribution, and in the morning, I could wake up and eat breakfast and be outside to swim long before my family would arrive.

There were moments when I loved going to Michigan, and this was one of them. Besides everything that was wrong with it, the cottage could still be a fun place to be. It may not have been Disneyland, but it was better than nothing, and I made the most of it when I could.

That night, my cousins and I plotted what we would do with all the extra time we'd have together in the morning. We could go fishing, which amounted to standing at the end of the long, rickety pier that jutted from the shore into the shallow water in front of the cottage and waiting for a fish the size of a baby's shoe to decide life wasn't worth living. (I will never understand the thrill of fishing. At its very best, it's an activity that ends with a vicious struggle to reel in something you can easily buy at a supermarket. And then what? You take a picture with it? So you can make that picture the cover of your dating profile? Nobody is impressed with your ability to catch a fish. Turtles can catch fish. Nobody is trying to fuck a turtle.) Besides fishing, we could also go tubing, but tubing is only fun for about five minutes, until you hit a small wave and are violently catapulted into the air and come crashing down into the water like you're diving into a plate of frozen steaks, and suddenly there is water in orifices you didn't know existed. The only real option was to go for an early boat ride, and the only boat we could operate ourselves was the paddleboat, the water version of a bicycle, really just exercise disguised as fun. But still, we could ride it out to the middle of the lake where the water was deepest and jump in without fear of getting grabbed by anything lurking at the bottom.

So that morning, we all got up and threw on our swim trunks. After breakfast, we took the requisite two hours to slather on SPF 1000 sunblock, a ritual that always proved pointless for our pale Anglo skin.

I walked the fifty yards to the lake while I waited for my

cousins to finish smearing their pasty bodies, and waded a few feet into the water around the paddleboat. It was a beautiful morning—crisp, you might say, if you used words like that to describe the air and not a potato chip. The water felt brisk and refreshing, like swimming in a cold glass of lemonade, if that's your thing. It was the type of morning that made coming to this mess of a place worth it.

And then I took a single step into the water and the beauty of the morning came rupturing to a close. I felt a shooting pain in the bottom of my foot—once again, stepping had proven to be my greatest weakness; if only I owned a pair of shoes—and when I lifted my foot from the water to look, there was a slice, almost two inches in length, along my heel. I'd stepped directly onto a shard of glass and cut my heel almost wide open.

If I'd had the fortitude in the moment, there are plenty of people I'd like to have cursed, namely myself for daring to think going outside was ever, *ever* a good idea, but also whichever redneck, yahoo motherfucker decided to throw a motherfucking broken bottle of shitty beer into a fucking lake. I can imagine plenty of terrible things a person can do, like getting a tattoo of another person's face or drinking even a single swig of milk a second after the expiration date, but throwing a shard of jagged glass into the shallow part of a lake is among the worst of them, and not just because I happened to step on it, even though that maybe had something to do with it. Seriously, fuck you, sir or madam. I hope one day you step on something even worse, like a really hot beach or one of those extra-long Legos.

I was surprisingly calm in the moment, perhaps because the water was washing away the blood, and I limped the fifty yards back up to the house, where my aunt was sitting on the deck drinking her morning coffee.

"Uhh, Auntie Bonnie," I said. "I think I cut my foot."

By then, my aunt Bonnie was well used to my injuries. Virtually every time I was left in her charge, I'd come limping back to her with some broken bone, sprain, burn, or open wound. It became a running joke in the family that she should refuse to look after me because I posed too much of an insurance risk. My injuries were so routine that she barely blinked when I told her I'd cut my foot.

"I'll go get a Band-Aid," she sighed without looking up at me.

I don't know why I didn't stop her and say, "Listen, lady, there's no time for Band-Aids, we need Super Glue and maybe also a miracle," but she was a pharmacist, which is basically a doctor, so I trusted her. Either way, she was gone before I could say anything. A few minutes later, she returned with a bandage.

By then, there was a small pool of blood forming beneath me, and her eyes widened ever so slightly as she got closer, in that way that adults' eyes tend to widen when they realize things are more fucked than they'd originally realized, but don't want to admit it out loud.

"Oh," she said with a kind of forced composure. "You *really* cut it, huh?"

She tried to say it calmly, but I have a knack for picking up on the panic in people's voices, especially when they're staring at an open wound in my body, and I could tell what she really meant to say was, "We'll be lucky if we can save the leg."

She used a water bottle to clear the blood away, and tried

to see how deep the cut was, but when she peeled back the skin for just a moment, she let out the faintest of gasps. I could see what she saw, too. A dark spot, maybe a piece of dirt—that lake was filthy, after all, hence the broken beer bottle—but it looked more like part of a vein, maybe even an artery, and even though I don't entirely know the difference between a vein and an artery, or whether there are even arteries in your feet (who knows!), it looked bad, like what you'd imagine cutting an artery would look like. I went pale. The blood kept coming.

"Let's just call your mom," Aunt Bonnie said, but I knew what she really meant: "Think about what you'd like to say to your mother before you die."

I could hear her dialing the phone. By now, my parents would be on their way to the cottage, the car bounding down the highway with bottles of beer rattling in the seat where I would've been uncomfortably squished otherwise.

"Hey, Deb," she said almost calmly when my mother answered. "Are you guys close?"

"Almost," my mother said. "Why? Is everything OK?" Debbie, always assuming the worst has happened.

"Yep, everything's good," Aunt Bonnie said. Even though she really meant, "You left your dainty, fragile piece-of-shit son with me, and now he's going to die."

I could tell she didn't want to get my mother worried, especially not when there was nothing she could do, not from the highway at least. And to be perfectly honest, I was fine with her not knowing. My mother is a notoriously worried woman, and I knew the second she learned I'd nearly cut off my foot, she'd go on and on about how we never should have been allowed near that water without military-grade protective body suits, at least three adult supervisors, and a written permission slip from a medical professional. My mother absolutely insisted that we all wear water shoes, those disgustingly ugly mesh clogs that meld to your feet the second they get wet. I hated water shoes. I hated that they filled with dirt and sand and gave my feet a rash. I hated that they made my feet feel heavy and dull. I hated the hideous colors they were designed in. And I hated knowing that I would now almost certainly never hear the end of it.

Aunt Bonnie looked at me the way you look at a bird that's flown into a window and broken its wing, the look that says, "You'll be dead within the hour, you poor idiot."

"Let's go to the bathroom and see if we can clean it out," she said.

And so, I hobbled to the bathroom, my cousins now crowded around me, and placed my bloody stump under the bathtub faucet. Aunt Bonnie bent down and tried spreading the wound so the water could clean inside of it. I could tell she was trying to see if the dark spot was going away, if it was only a piece of dirt, and not an open artery spilling out the last of my life force. The spot wouldn't go away. The bleeding had somewhat abated, but it hadn't stopped entirely. We wrapped it in paper towels.

Aunt Bonnie picked up the phone again. I could tell her concern was growing. She'd had a perfect record so far, in terms of making sure I hadn't died, but this time was shaping up differently. I mean, all told, even if I *had* died (spoiler alert: I didn't die), her record still would've been pretty good. One death out of mostly not dying is not too bad.

She dialed my mother again, and I could hear her answer.

"Hey, Deb," Aunt Bonnie said, less convincingly calm this time. "Almost here?"

"We're five minutes away," my mother said. "Something's wrong, I can tell."

"Well," Aunt Bonnie said. "There's been an incident."

A moment passed while my mother waited for news that I'd been decapitated, castrated, or worse.

"Well, Matthew stepped on a piece of glass, and uh . . . he might have cut an artery."

"AN ARTERY!?" I could hear my mother scream through the phone.

"Yeah, maybe just a little bit," Aunt Bonnie said.

But my mother was already crying. My father, you could hear, was yelling from the driver's seat, "Goddammit! It's always fucking something!"

"Oh, God. Why are you crying?" my brother was asking from the backseat.

"Auntie Bonnie said he cut an artery!" my mother was sobbing. "Do you want me to scream like he's doing?"

The dog, I'm sure, vomited one last time.

This is how my family reacts to news.

A few minutes later, the car came shrieking down the gravel road. My mother leapt from the passenger seat, and before I had a chance to say hello, I'd been swept into the backseat, boxes of groceries tossed onto the pavement to make room for my failing body, and we were speeding back down the gravel road to the emergency room.

. . .

"You just need a few stitches" is what the doctor said when he'd finally had a chance to look me over.

"Are you sure, Doctor?" my mother was asking. "Are you sure he hasn't cut an artery?"

I would make fun of her for questioning the doctor on something that would be obvious to a doctor, but then again, this was small-town Michigan. The hospital was in between a Dairy Queen and a Blockbuster Video.

"Um. Yes," he said. "He'd be dead if he cut an artery."

A tetanus shot, a handful of stitches, and a bagful of prescription painkillers later, we were driving back to the cottage, the open green fields of Michigan passing by the window.

I'd like to say I found a new appreciation for those views, the kind of appreciation that people who have faced death feel. I'd like to say I looked out that window and said something profound, something that someone who's really gone through stuff says, like "You never know how much you've been missing until you almost lose it all."

But I couldn't say that.

All I could muster, before the pain drugs took over, was one simple sentence:

"This never would've happened if we just went to fucking Disneyland."

ON THE TERRORS OF NATURE

I've never understood people who actually enjoy being outdoors. I understand you can't exactly avoid going outside. I admit I leave my apartment for ten minutes every day to retrieve sandwiches and cookies to drag back to my lair. But I certainly don't have fun doing it. Outside is where the sun's piercing rays sear my skin. Outside is where spiders breed and plot ways to penetrate my kitchen. Outside is where bears live. Like actual bears that roam around waiting to rip your arms and legs off and eat them like stale chicken wings. If I didn't need nutrition or occasional sunlight to survive, rest assured my apartment door would stay permanently bolted.

My distaste of nature began as early as I can remember, during one disastrous weekend my family spent RVing in Wisconsin. In their youthful naiveté, my parents not only enjoyed being outdoors but actively sought time to be outside exclusively, like some kind of forest animals, content with only the trees and a bonfire and a fully equipped RV. I was never on board with the concept of the RV, even as an infant, when I still regularly shit my pants. If you're putting an entire house on wheels just to drive it into the woods, why don't you just stay in the fucking house? You can call it a recreational vehicle all you want, but an RV will always be the vehicle you don't want to drive behind on the highway because there's a 100 percent chance that an infant child is giving you the middle finger from the rear window. I was that infant child. And that middle finger was my cry for help. I like to point out this fact to clarify that I myself was never an RVer, simply the child of RVers and an unwitting participant in the culture of RVing. And yes, RVing is not just an activity, but an entire culture, with a rich history of camping in Walmart parking lots and dumping buckets of piss and shit on the side of the American interstate highway system. It's a beautiful culture, respected by many, and disrespected by many more.

My parents never owned an RV, but our family friend Sue owned one, and that was good enough for us. Sue was an old, sprightly woman who worked with my parents years earlier at the department store where they met. (Yes, my parents met working at a department store. I am a child of coupons and cheap garments.) By the time I was born, Sue was already widowed and retired, and spent her free time driving out into the wilderness to enjoy nature. I loved Sue. She had a nasty sense of humor—most of the time, I didn't know what she was laughing about, but I laughed along with her anyway. She had a bunch of cactuses in her house that were taller than I was and a full basement with a pool table and a bunch of paintings of clowns that when the lights were turned off I'm pretty sure sprang to life to feast on cubes of beef and carrion that Sue flung to them from upstairs. She was a quirky old broad who would do stuff like that.

"The camper," as it was affectionately called, was always parked in Sue's driveway. We were never allowed inside of it when we were at Sue's house—just like we only got to go to the basement while the clown paintings were sleeping—but I'd always wondered what happened inside of it. I was probably only four or five at the time, but I remember being fascinated by the idea that someone would actually want to fit an entire house onto a big old bus and take it into the wilderness for fun. But of course, we soon got invited to go with Sue on a camping trip, and I would discover exactly why fitting your entire house onto a bus is perhaps not the most ideal arrangement.

This was before that fucking *Tiny House Hunters* show on HGTV fetishized the idea of living in a cardboard box. No offense to people who live in cardboard boxes, but I prefer to sleep in a bed that's more than twelve inches away from the toilet, and I resent the entire Home and Gardens Television network for suggesting I should want otherwise.

So one weekend, my mom, dad, brother, and I drove for what felt like an entire day to get to Sue's camper in Wisconsin (I'm sure it was only four hours, possibly less), and parked in a campground near a lake. I remember the excitement I felt when I got out of the car and the immediate disappointment I felt when I saw where we had parked.

The "campground" was nothing more than a patch of dirt no larger than a strip mall parking lot, next to a lake so overrun with tree roots and algae, you could barely tell where the shore ended and the water began. Even if you wanted to jump in, there'd be no way to return without climbing through bushes and muck.

You'd think, as an infant, I wouldn't have had the worldly experience to distinguish a bad outdoors experience from a good one. But I knew this was shit. "At least there's a swimming pool on the campground," my mother tried to assure us. But when we walked by the pool to investigate, we discovered a hole full of green, cloudy water and a single used diaper floating listlessly in the center, crushing all of my hopes and dreams.

When we got inside the camper to clean up after our day-long journey to Wisconsin, we discovered that the water supply along this particular lake was apparently high in hydrogen sulfide gas, causing what is otherwise known as "sulfur water," or water that smells like someone shit out a dozen deviled eggs and then sprayed it with the blood of a dozen other deviled eggs that had been freshly killed earlier that morning.

They say smell can be the strongest trigger for memory, which is perhaps why I remember this weekend so vividly over two decades later. Because it smelled like death the entire time.

Honestly, I don't remember why we didn't turn right around and drive back that minute. I'm sure I used my limited vocabulary to advocate for that very action. But being an RVer means never saying no to a challenge, so apparently we spent an entire weekend bathing in boiled egg water and just dealing with it. I asked my mother years later why the hell we didn't turn around and go straight back home when we turned on the faucet and the cursed souls of egg demons poured from the tap, and she said we stayed to "enjoy each other's company," because apparently some people are satisfied by nothing more than conversation with other humans and are willing to overlook the minor inconveniences of tainted water and diaper pools. And yet the sulfur water was hardly the only terrible thing about that weekend. It was all terrible. There were bugs. It was itchy. We spent the whole weekend sitting by a campfire, where I learned that my body is extremely allergic to mosquitoes, which is a thing you can actually be allergic to, because every one of their tiny clawing bites turned into a giant welt. My only toy that weekend was a fly swatter, which I used to great effect, but still. I was being literally eaten alive in a tiny house car with nothing but egg water to soothe my wounds. On top of all that, I had the distinct privilege, as the youngest camper that weekend, of sleeping on the breakfast table. In true RV fashion, the surface of the kitchen table was detachable and, with a few maneuvers, turned into a bed. Imagine a restaurant booth, but take away the supporting leg and put the tabletop flush between the seats, and voilà, you got yourself an RV bed. At least that's how they sold it to me when they told me I was sleeping on a breakfast table. Once you get over the initial excitement of getting to sleep where you eat your Froot Loops, you realize you're sleeping on a literal table, which is perhaps the least appealing of sleeping surfaces. I was a kid, dehydrated from a scarcity of egg-free drinking water and sapped of all my blood from thirsty mosquitoes, so I'm sure I passed out.

When we finally escaped on Sunday evening, the rest of my family apparently content enough with a weekend of one another's company, I spent the entire car ride home scratching my mosquito bites into bloody gashes and cursing the outdoors forever. Nature, I knew then more than ever, was nothing more than an itchy, putrid adventure into hell itself.

.   .   .

The older I got, and the more time I spent ignoring the outdoors, the more my distaste for nature evolved into genuine fear. Do I wish I could've grown into one of those burly men from the Discovery Channel who can make his own venison jerky and chase hurricanes and put out forest fires? Sure. But only because they get to spend a lot of very intimate time with other burly men in scant clothing, and I'm about that life. But alas, I grew into a true nature sissy, terrified not only by being outside but by what nature could do to me while I was indoors.

The very earliest dream I can remember was a nightmare I had when I couldn't have been more than a few years old. I was playing outside when, in seconds, the sky turned violently gray and then pitch-black and I woke up in a pile of snot and tears and probably urine if we're being honest, and it took a few packages of frozen waffles to console me.

There were no tall buildings in the suburbs where I grew up, so anytime there was bad weather, you could see the angry dark sky for miles and miles and it always made me feel so small and defenseless. We lived on the periphery of the tornado belt, after all. Every year at school, we'd have tornado drills, where we'd crawl into the hallways and roll into balls against the wall, and sometimes, if you didn't get into the hallway quick enough, you'd have to start forming a row *behind* the kids who were already against the wall, so your tiny face was up in some other kid's butt—but that was the price we paid for staying safe. I'd seen *The Wizard of Oz* enough times to know that tornadoes weren't fucking around. I mean, sure, a tornado flung Dorothy to a land of tiny dancing homosexuals, which I wouldn't have been opposed to, but also, her house literally killed someone! I wasn't about to be the next person with fabulous shoes to get killed in a tornado.

And yes, that's an entirely normal fear to have. Long before I was born, my mother's cousin was killed in a tornado in the next town over, and perhaps it was my mother's constant repetition of that story, or perhaps it was something deeper, but every summer, my fear of storms got worse and worse.

One summer, my mother was mowing the lawn with an electric mower that was plugged into an outlet with a long, winding extension cord. It started pouring rain and she didn't stop mowing, and I went outside and stood next to her literally screaming my eyes out over the claps of thunder because I was sure she was about to be electrocuted to death. (Which is a concern I would maintain today. Not the brightest idea on her part.) I was sobbing convulsively, convinced that if she weren't electrocuted, she'd definitely be struck by lightning or swept up by a tornado that was obviously headed directly to our house. She finished the job, which I'm sure I made ten times more difficult by standing in her path, and somehow she was never electrocuted to death. But it remains possibly the most scared I've ever been.

There was one storm in particular, probably around 1998, that struck while we were at a public pool. And yes, before you judge us, we went to public pools. We didn't get a fancy aboveground pool in our backyard until the 2000s, so we were forced to go swimming in public like animals. It was a balmy, cloudy day, but otherwise storm-less, and the entire family went. About halfway through the day, a lifeguard spotted lightning and made everybody get out of the water until the storm clouds passed over, which was perfectly fine, because it was lunchtime, and I was hungry.

While we sat unpeeling our peanut butter sandwiches from their damp plastic wraps, I looked up and saw a sinister cloud billowing toward us, a plume of green-gray smoke. I'd seen plenty of storm clouds before, but no cloud moved as menacingly as this one, like a thick snake uncoiling rapidly above us. Suddenly, the winds whipped violently around us, the rain came down like bullets, and everybody was running in a different direction. "This is the big one!" my mother screamed. A sign from the hot dog stand came loose and flew down and hit the person next to me in the head. I stood up, threw away my entire sandwich, and ran for the closest structure: the women's bathroom. We all darted inside and clung to the concrete walls, which shook against the wind. I turned to find my older cousin sobbing uncontrollably with a hot dog in his hand. His body was convulsing, but he kept eating. It remains the most hilarious, yet terrifying moment of my childhood.

Eventually, the storm passed and we all survived. But a giant tree was literally ripped from its roots and thrown into the shallow end of the pool where we'd been swimming a half hour earlier.

So to anyone who says that my fear of nature is unfounded, that I'm a grown-ass man who lives in a city where the most dangerous wildlife are dog-sized cockroaches and rat kings, that your chances of getting bit by a radioactive spider or swept away in a tornado, especially in New York City, are far less than the chances of slipping in the shower as a result of dancing too hard to a Spice Girls song and trying to finish my sub sandwich, know that my terror is well-rooted in a history of what I consider dramatic near-deaths, and I'm lucky to be alive. You can take your outdoors propaganda to the next fool unfazed by the presence of vicious cyclones and bloodthirsty bears, and when he gets ripped apart and thrown to another state, I'll be inside, under three layers of sheets and blankets, whispering over and over, "I told you so."

ON TEENAGERS AND WHY THEY'RE THE WORST

There is no species on earth that strikes as much fear in my heart as the American teenager. And yes, I'm singling out Americans, because I'm pretty sure teenagers don't even exist in other countries. In France, they go right from being babies to being cigarette-smoking, coffee-swilling adult men with lush chest hair, and that's not even an offensive description, because everybody in France would agree with me. I have a friend who's French and she says so. But we're talking about America here, where babies grow up to be even bigger babies, and all we really get along the way is incurable anxiety and crippling student loan debt. We're the only country in the world where children are coddled for a full twenty-five to forty years, and teenagers, falling right in the middle of that incubation period, are given free rein to wreak terror on society.

I, for one, am not a fan of teenagers, if you couldn't tell, and not just because they know more about sex than I do.

Teenagers are objectively terrifying. They gather in parking lots and behind gas stations and under bridges, plotting ways to destroy the world, and I don't trust them even a little bit. You would think that their lanky, underdeveloped bodies would be vulnerable, like a snake after it molts its skin. But somehow the mixture of teenage angst and hormones festers to create an unpredictable beast unseen anywhere else in nature. It astounds me that we actively encourage teenagers to become babysitters. *Babysitters. As in, the people we trust to sit on our nation's babies.* "Oh sure, you can barely control your own disgusting body, but go ahead and take care of my completely defenseless infant. Also, here's some car keys, because you may only be sixteen and your brain isn't fully developed yet, but I trust you implicitly to operate my four-thousand-pound vehicle." Honestly, I miss the old days, when everybody died peacefully of cholera at the ripe old age of thirteen, surrounded by their grandchildren.

But let's focus. Teenagers are disgusting. Their bodies produce fragrances and flavors that could unclog even the most congested of sinuses. Their skin is sticky, they smell, and they have absolutely no regard for basic garbage disposal. I'll be honest, I don't know how my mother managed to live with my father and two teenage boys for a full decade without burning down the house the second she found a questionable tissue stuck to the carpet. Ecologists could write volumes about the communities of organisms that lived in my teenage bedsheets alone. I went into my brother's bedroom once and saw a pillowcase physically carry itself across the room to feed on the bottom of a nearly empty bowl of cereal. That's real. That really happened. Some say he still sleeps on the same unwashed sheets today. (Me. I say that.)

Worst of all, the modern American teenager is merciless in attitude. Perhaps it's because they don't yet realize life will one day utterly destroy them, or perhaps it's because they do, but teenagers have the unique ability to emotionally ravage you without lifting a single finger. And I'm not talking about the gangs of them that wait outside Dunkin' Donuts every morning to taunt me for buying three boxes of assorted Munchkins in sweatpants. I'm talking about teenagers on the Internet.

I happen to make my living writing on the Internet. It's a meager profession, and I have to sell my body on the side to make ends meet, but generally speaking, it comes with very little risk. The only workplace hazards I face regularly are: masturbating too many times in a row until it starts to kinda hurt, taking too long of a shower and turning into a lifeless prune, and choking to death on an egg roll because I don't have a strapping, muscled boyfriend to perform the Heimlich on me. But I would take any of those things over the real danger I face every day: the cutting insult from a mean-as-hell teenage girl.

Because I've chosen to write about my interests, which happen to include attractive young men, pop music, boy-band stars, and television programs featuring all of the above, I've somehow attracted a regular audience of intensely feral teenage girls, who collectively make up a stronger offensive force than all of the world's militaries combined. Seriously, if teenage girls decide to organize one day, there's literally nothing we can do to stop them. Just go on the Internet and look up pictures from any Justin Bieber concert. There are girls bursting through steel barricades, dismembering security guards, and feasting on one another's flesh. And this is all before we've even allowed them to vote.

When they like you, of course, there's no problem. In fact, I've had plenty of perfectly rewarding interactions with teenage girls on the Internet, which is a sentence that would normally land a grown man like myself on *Dateline*, but it's OK, because we're preying on Zac Efron and not one another. But say one wrong thing, however innocuous yet hilarious you think it may be, and you become Teenage Girl Enemy Number One. And let me tell you, teenage angst knows no borders. I've been yelled at in more languages and from more countries than I knew existed. All for daring to say that a boy-band member (who shall remain nameless because I value my life) should perhaps cut his hair an inch shorter, and possibly consider using shampoo.

And teenage girls don't hold back. I'm chubby, gay, pale, and a whole decade older than most of them, which means I might as well wear a sign that says, "Hello, fellow Internet users, please destroy my entire life." I've been called an untoasted marshmallow; an old loaf of Wonder Bread; a slice of unbuttered toast (a lot of their insults are carb-based); a balding, middle-aged menace; someone who should go ahead and kill himself already; and my personal favorite, "Casper the faggot ghost," which would be offensive if it weren't so clever and nostalgic. (Kudos to today's youth for honoring a classic nineties movie. Also Human Casper was adorable, so fuck you, teens.)

Of course, I've angered a great many people on the Internet for a number of reasons. It's kind of impossible to exist on the Internet *without* angering at least 10 percent of the people who interact with you. But insults from teenage girls always seem to cut deepest.

I have a number of theories as to why this is true. Some would say society pressures girls into living up to impossible standards and turns them against one another at the earliest possible age, meaning they're literally prepared for war at all times and are likely to lash out at whatever target happens to provoke them at any given moment, which is usually me, a pasty gay who's writing about their favorite Jonas brother. It also doesn't help that I show up to their concerts and stand in front of them and scream louder than they do, but I can't help that my hormones are just as aggressive as theirs. But the theory that seems most true is the simplest: teenagers are assholes.

So let's talk about teenage assholes. Not like, literal teenage assholes. If the FBI is reading this, please don't arrest me for typing "teenage assholes." It's not what you think. I'm talking about teenage assholes, like teenagers who *are* assholes. Not teenagers who *have* assholes. Although probably every teenager has an asshole, so I guess we're talking about teenagers who do technically have assholes, but we're not talking about their literal assholes, we're talking about how they *are* assholes. I'm glad we cleared that up. Anyway, let's talk about teenage assholes.

I was a teenage asshole. And not just *any* teenage asshole, but the worst *kind* of teenage asshole: the self-righteous, *nerdy* teenage asshole. Yes, nerds can be assholes, too, and sometimes, they're even worse assholes than the other types of assholes, because they grow up thinking that the world owes them something for making them a nerd. I would've saved myself a lot of trouble if I could have gone back and told this to my child self. I would've taken that scruffy ginger nerd by the collar and shook him till his glasses fell off. It's what he deserved. But alas, I became the asshole I would so despise.

In third grade, I fashioned myself a budding sociologist, and laid out what I believed to be an irrefutable system by which I could categorize the entire third-grade class. There were, according to my scientific observations, three distinct social echelons into which every one of my classmates could be placed. There were the popular kids, of course—the girls with pretty hair, and the boys who could run farther than a hundred feet without bending over in agonizing pain. There were the obviously unpopular kids—the girl who sat inside during recess to read books and the boy who brought his pet mouse to the playground in his jacket pocket. (Listen, I know these are cruel and arbitrary factors, but really, what the fuck kind of child brings a mouse to school?) And then there was the third, in-between group of kids who clearly weren't popular, but weren't exactly unpopular, who simply existed beneath the radar, somewhere in the middle of it all. I'll let you guess which group I placed myself in.

This is, of course, a complete asshole's way of thinking, and a cheap way for an insecure little shit to convince himself he's not at the bottom of the totem pole. (And sure, I was, like, the class clown or whatever, and that counted for something, but still. Dick move.)

I guess it was important for my nerdy, chubby, insecure self to have a place, even if that place was a fantasyland I created in the middle of the social order. I could never be one of the quirky, carefree kids who didn't give a flying fuck about what other people thought of him. I cared deeply about what everybody else thought, and even if I wasn't the most popular, it mattered that there was an identity that I fit into.

And this way of thinking stayed with me well into high school, where my nerdy asshole-ness could reach its fullest form. I needed an identity to cling to, after all, even if that identity was to be an asshole nerd. So that's what I became.

There are all types of nerds in the world. There are nerds who play wizard card games and nerds who play chess and nerds who read comic books and nerds who know way too much about *Star Wars*. I was a math and science nerd. When I started high school in 2004, I tested high enough on my entrance exams to skip freshman-level honors algebra and jump right into sophomore-level honors geometry, which would be impressive if this wasn't the public school system in suburban Chicago, where a literal monkey could have broken the curve. I don't know if you've ever been to a public school, especially one in Chicago, but it's basically prison, but with paler food and more bathroom sex. Seriously. One day, we found a loose DVD of heterosexual pornography on the cafeteria floor. Straight porn! Where we ate! Disgusting.

Anyway. I happened to be one of two thirteen-year-olds who outsmarted the system, and I started my first day of high school a virtual prodigy.

Now, it's not easy being a boy genius. Everybody assumes

it's all fun and games and strippers and cocaine. "You'll be so popular," they say. "All the ladies will love you! You'll grow up and Russell Crowe will play you in the movies!" But let's be real. Being a boy genius is hard work. You have to get new glasses every two months because your eyes are so terrible. You have to bring candies to the teachers so they know you're a suck-up. And legally, you're required to fail gym class.

But something in my brain responded to being called smart. It made me feel good that I was the smart kid. It had its negative connotations, but at least I knew who I was. So I leaned into it.

I carried around heavy books because it made me feel smarter. My backpack weighed over a hundred pounds and stuck out at least ten inches from my back, and I'm sure it led to long-term spinal degeneration, but it was worth it for the extra time I got to spend studying. I studied aggressively for tests because I needed to get not just an A, but the highest score in class. There weren't enough periods in the day for the number of AP and honors classes I wanted to fit into my schedule. Literally. I had to petition the administration to let me skip my lunch period to add on AP Biology. I was literally begging the school to let me sacrifice the one good thing in the world.

And here's where I became an asshole, or at least started my journey toward asshole-dom. I prized good grades over any meaningful relationships. I wanted to be the smartest. I didn't like sharing my notes or even studying with other people. Group projects were my personal hell. (Seriously, fuck you if you ever asked me to cheat. Some girl tricked me into sharing my binder of meticulous notes, which I know for a fact she straight up photocopied before giving back to me.) Every time we took a test, I'd create an impenetrable tent out of my shoulders and arms so nobody could catch even a glance at my answers and steal my precious knowledge.

By the way, children, if you're reading this, cheating is totally fine. Nobody cares. As long as you cheat *together*. Don't give anybody your answers unless there's something in it for you. The bargaining and socializing skills you'll learn in these transactions will be far more useful to you in the future than any actual knowledge you're losing by cheating. So go ahead.

Eventually, the grind broke me. I was constantly sarcastic, bitter, snappy, and worse, perpetually exhausted, which made me even more insufferable to be around. I went to the doctor for fatigue, and that's when he first suggested that maybe I wasn't just overworked but depressed, which not only makes your brain feel like it would constantly be better off with a nap, but also that you're somehow not good enough.

Regardless of the source of my insufferableness, there's nothing worse than a teenager who thinks he knows more than everybody else. My mother would ask me to clean up a pile of junk I'd left on the stairs and I'd dramatically shout back something like, "You know I could be a drug dealer, right?! I could be out on the streets doing all kinds of marijuana right now. But no. I'm wasting my time being an honors child." It's like she didn't even appreciate the bumper sticker I got for her every semester.

Applying to college only made things worse. There's nothing like cornering a child who's already racked with hormones, acne, and itchy pubic hair and pressuring them into sacrificing their sanity for higher education. I mean, I was a teenager! I could barely be trusted to stay at home by myself without accidentally setting fire to a frozen pizza. And now colleges were like, "It's no big deal. We just need you to figure out what you want to do with the next sixty-five years of your life."

There's a thing that happens when you're kinda smart in public school, and that is, you get fed into a machine that demands that you try your very hardest to make it to college. You have to get the best grades and join eleven clubs and be good at sports and speak five languages and nurse wounded animals back to health. And I fell into it hard.

The whole process of going to college is fucked. First, you have to pass a bunch of tests to prove that you know enough to even be able to go to college. Then you have to know where the fuck you wanna go. Then you have to write approximately seventeen personal essays, and all the example essays they give you are by people who almost died of cancer or cured AIDS in their hometown.

Neither of my parents went to college, and as much as they wanted to help me through the process, they didn't know how, and it only made my teenage asshole self more resentful and self-entitled. "Fine," I thought. "I'll figure this shit out myself. Just get ready to write a very large student loan check every month for the next twenty to fifty years and we'll totally be OK."

Making it even worse: my archrival, Alonso Garcia. That's not his real name, but I want you to know it's close to his real name, so don't go thinking I made up some fake-sounding Mexican name just because he was Mexican. Anyway, Alonso was the cooler, multicultural version of me. Besides being a fellow boy genius, he was a college admissions counselor's wet dream: he was a soccer and volleyball star, he emigrated from Guadalajara when he was six years old and could read and write fluently in both English and Spanish, and he was socially adept enough to be charming with absolutely everybody. I'm sure he cured babies with cancer in his spare time. Alonso and I were friends, but our friendship was infused with a potent rivalry. Who would get a better score on the ACT? Who would get into the better college? And who would be valedictorian? There could only be one and we were both after it. (And by both of us, I mean me, and Alonso just happened to be there, too. I think, in retrospect, he got more fulfillment out of watching me try to best him than from actually winning. But I cared. Oh, did I care.)

Of course, Alonso was always ahead. He scored higher on the ACT, got into all the best schools, and was our valedictorian. He gave some beautiful, bilingual valedictory speech that I probably would've remembered if I hadn't been so busy seething in anger at the time. He's married now with kids and a job and everything, and I'm just here writing about how I hate children. But at the time, Alonso kept me on my toes, and I was determined to nerd out as hard as I could.

So, in addition to taking every class I could, I insisted on joining every club there was, which, according to most kids and also movies about high school, is only a thing that high schoolers do when they want to take long trips to state tournaments so they can stay overnight in hotel rooms with other high schoolers and also do dirty stuff on the bus ride there. I, not surprisingly, was in it for the game. Yes, I was a mathlete, and yes, before you ask, I was indeed our team's MVP. I was also editor of the school paper and, for good measure, treasurer of the Art Club, which was actually just a bunch of closeted gay children who spent their afternoons pretending they were simply eccentric and not also homosexual.

Perhaps most illustratively, though, I was president of the Science Club, a group whose primary purpose was to give nerds like me a place to escape getting beat up after school. We spent half of the year building what's called a Rube Goldberg machine, which is basically the game Mouse Trap, a ridiculous contraption that takes a thousand ridiculous steps involving marbles and slides and falling shoes and buckets that all happen one after the other like falling dominoes. Each year, there's a national Rube Goldberg competition, and nerdy engineer-lings in science clubs across the country gather their pimply faces together to build a dumb machine that does a dumb thing. And you better believe our nerdy asses were in the game.

The task this particular year was to build a machine that could assemble a simple hamburger: a (precooked) patty, lettuce, tomato, ketchup, mustard, and pickles, with a bottom and top bun. Now, to remind you again, we were a science club in a public school in Chicago. Well, technically the suburbs, but still. We weren't working with titanium steel or precious oaks and marbles. We could afford a box of rubber bands, a pile of toothpicks, and a heap of rotted wood someone's dad left at the side of the garage. Somehow, we had to turn this into a working structure that could assemble an edible hamburger.

We spent months working on this thing, sketching diagrams and building prototypes and causing a not insignificant number of small but terrifying table fires. And finally, under what I can only imagine was my stellar leadership, we built ourselves a clunky monstrosity that put together a goddamn burger. I mean, *barely*, and only about 10 percent of the time. But we were proud of it nonetheless.

Here's how it worked: our creation was carnival-themed, with the bottom bun sitting on a carousel in the center of the structure. When the machine launched, the carousel would start to spin, and each of the ingredients would fall neatly into place on top of the bun—the patty fell through a Plinko-style tower that triggered a hammer that smashed a bottle of ketchup that set off a bell that triggered a butcher knife that swung onto a head of lettuce, and so on and so forth until we had a fully constructed burger glistening in the center.

At least that was the idea. We were ten sixteen-year-olds with nothing but hot-glue guns, moldy sesame seed buns, and feral hormones. Our machine worked in theory, but more often than not, a string snapped here, a knife flung there, our machine would start smoking under duress, and we'd devolve into a battle over who fucked it up this time. There were days when we thought bringing this mess to a competition would surely bring more embarrassment than glory, and we considered letting it burn itself to the ground.

But by sheer force of will, we got our beautiful burger baby to cooperate just long enough to do what it had to do. And so, on the morning of the state championship in downtown Chicago, we lugged it onto a bus and brought her in. And by the way, I don't know if you've ever been on a bus with a bunch of teenage nerds and a pile of cheap wood that's been covered in raw beef and cheese for five months, but it's not pretty. The fact that we survived that bus ride was a miracle unto itself.

But the biggest miracle of all was what happened when we got there. Because guess what? We won that shit. We won it all. Good ol' Burger Machine did her very best, and we clobbered the other nerds and their measly attempts at engineering perfection. In retrospect, we more than likely won because the other Chicago schools were even more ridiculously underfunded than us. But still. We fucking did it.

A week later, we went to nationals, a contest so highly prestigious and respected that they held it in none other than an empty warehouse in West Lafayette, Indiana. We went in with as much confidence as ten virgins hot off a stunning upset victory can muster in a situation like this—and, as you would probably suspect, got utterly and horrendously destroyed. Good ol' Burger Machine just couldn't survive the bumpy two-hour bus ride from Chicago to West Lafayette, and lost her magic. Besides, it was bound to happen when you pit a Chicago public school (from the suburbs, but still) against a bunch of high schools with words like "institute" in their names. We didn't have a chance.

But the week in between our victory and loss was a fantastic one. Yes, it was the nerdiest accomplishment possible. And no, we didn't get a pep rally or anything. But still, victory validated our dweeby existences, and gave me even more fuel to continue my nerdy conquests.

Later that same year, still fueled by Rube Goldberg glory, the Science Club entered the Chicago South Suburban Science Invitational, a regional competition of veritable geeks in all areas of science from all over Chicagoland. It was generally less nerdy than it sounds. There were contests for the strongest Popsicle-stick bridge, the lightest paper airplane, and the farthest-traveling mousetrap-powered vehicle. Our school entered students in every category for the broadest possible chance at victory. My category? Insect identification.

Now, I know what you're thinking. "Matt, you hate bugs." And even though I never said that and you just assumed it because I'm a giant gay pansy with absolutely no backbone, you are absolutely right. I hate bugs. I think they're gross and ungodly and responsible for billions of dollars in crop damage annually, and I refuse to support any broad group of the animal kingdom that plays even the smallest part in limiting my access to potatoes. But listen. Duty calls. And when duty requires that you spend an entire night of your precious teenage years making and studying flash cards to identify which of the twenty-nine taxonomic orders of insects a butterfly belongs to, you fucking do it. (It's Lepidoptera, by the way, you moron.) I stayed up all night studying those flash cards, until I could classify a bumblebee with my eyes closed and my hands tied behind my back, and I walked into the Chicago South Suburban Science Invitational Insect Identification Contest like a mounted knight enters his field of battle. Twenty minutes later, I walked out a christened insect king. First place. In fact, I would've gotten a perfect score if the exam proctor had conceded that what he believed was a true bug (order: Hemiptera) was obviously just an unconvincing beetle (order: Coleoptera). But that man was an idiot and a coward. And guess who walked out of there with a first place blue ribbon and twenty-five-dollar Applebee's gift card? Not him.

By now you understand quite well that my nerdiness had gotten out of control. I had become merciless. I was an Almighty Nerd, my identity unquestioned. Anybody who stood in my way was subject to my wrath. Alonso. The preppy West Lafayette Institute kids. The insect man. They were all just people in my way.

So I understand now why teenagers are assholes. They know who they are. And we're just in their way.

But that doesn't mean I have to like them.

ON MY FIRST 100 DAYS AS PRESIDENT OF THE UNITED STATES

Nobody likes a complainer who doesn't put forth solutions. Or at least that's what people like to say when they get tired of listening to someone complain. The reality is, some things don't have solutions. That's why we're complaining about them. If I could fix half the shit I rant about, maybe I'd be a happier person and the world would be a better place. But like those old English guys said in that song that one time, "You don't always get what you want, so shut the fuck up, and stop complaining about people complaining." Or something like that. I don't really remember.

Nonetheless, I thought it wise to put forth an agenda—a working plan, if you will—of priorities that I might enact were I elected to a position to make them possible. I'm not saying this is the official declaration of my campaign for president, but if I *were* saying that, you might consider the following as the top of my to-do list.

DECREES I WOULD MAKE IMMEDIATELY AS PRESIDENT

1. Vice President Oprah Winfrey is to be appointed chief ego-booster to the president, and each day, she is to recite positive affirmations at me until I cry.

2. Any vegetable claiming to be a noodle, however thinly it may be sliced, is to be immediately exterminated, and any person who dare claims their vegetable is a noodle shall be sentenced to a life of hard labor in a pasta factory so they may understand that the true art of noodle-making will never include zucchini.

3. It shall be legal to violently murder any person who steps off an airplane, walks down the little hallway, and then stands right in front of the exit while they figure out where to go when there's a whole line of people waiting behind them.

4. All Starbursts will be pink Starbursts and all who protest in favor of yellow, orange, or red will be executed on the spot in the name of our Lord and Savior, the Almighty and Powerful Pink Starburst.

5. All public restroom stalls will be fitted with doors that span the entire stall, leaving no gap for creepy coworkers to leer at you mid–bowel movement, even though sometimes you understand the urge to see yourself pooping through the gap in the stall door.

6. All hot guys with cute dogs shall be enlisted in the president's secret reserves and called to serve at the pleasure of the president.

7. No reclining on airplanes because it's a dick move and it should never have been allowed in the first place. Honestly, the person behind you has like six inches of freedom in front of their face, and you're just gonna jerk back your cowardly spine and deprive them of air to breathe all for an extra *ten degrees* of comfort!? You're an asshole and so is everybody you love.

8. Babies are to be kept on silent at all times, and if one goes off in public, it shall be discarded.

9. Honking a car horn for longer than one second shall be considered a crime punishable by an unrelenting air horn directly to the eardrum until explosion.

10. All microwaves shall heat Hot Pockets to the perfect temperature, whereby the saucy center is heated evenly with the crusty surface.

11. Anybody who complains about not liking the Kardashians shall be banned from enjoying anything ever again. Sorry you didn't get famous for no reason. Let people enjoy their fucking reality TV show.

12. All squirrels are to be humanely euthanized and their meat is to be baked into pies given to disobedient children at Christmastime.

13. Any man who wishes to wear a V-neck in public must obtain written permission from the president personally. Applications for V-neck privileges should include pictures of the applicant wearing the requested garment(s). Applicants without defined pectorals and/or abdominals need not apply.

14. Every grocery store lane shall be a ten-items-or-less

lane, because nobody needs more than ten groceries at once.

15. People who say "I could care less" are to be banished to a remote island with people who say "irregardless."

16. Salad shall never be served as a meal.

17. All boxes of cereal shall cost one dollar, because it absolutely cannot cost eight dollars to make a box of Froot Loops.

18. Quinoa is banned because I don't trust it.

19. All professional sports must be performed in the nude, except NASCAR because I don't give a shit about NASCAR.

20. You know what, now that I think about it, let's just ban NASCAR. No NASCAR or any cars that go faster than, like, fifty miles per hour.

21. Listening to music out loud in public shall be a crime punishable by immediate flogging.

22. Nobody with gross feet is allowed to wear open-toed shoes, in private or otherwise.

23. Outside will be heated and air-conditioned.

24. Anybody who utters the words "Can I speak to the manager?" will be locked inside a dimly lit room overlooked by a two-way mirror. Inside this room will be a desk with a locked drawer. Inside this drawer will be a gun. Inside this gun will be a single bullet. The offender will be given three clues to find a key hidden inside the room. The key will unlock the drawer. If successful, the offender will retrieve the gun and then be faced with a choice: either shoot themselves or fire at the two-way mirror, shattering

the glass to find another room that may or may not lead them to safety. Unbeknownst to the offender, the second room will be occupied by a hungry mother grizzly bear recently separated from her newborn cub. If all goes well, the grizzly bear will rip the offender to shreds, whereupon the manager will enter to take the offender's question.

25. And finally: universal health care. I mean, c'mon. We can't let Canada have something that we don't.

ON TERRIBLE
FIRST JOBS

It should come as a surprise to absolutely no one that I don't like to work. They say, "Get a job doing what you love, and you'll never work a day in your life," or some bullshit like that, but I like doing absolutely nothing, and nobody's paying me to do that. Trust me, I've tried. If I could get paid for eating, I would do that, but at this point, people should be paying me to *stop* eating.

I should clarify, it's not because I'm lazy, or at least it's not *just* because I'm lazy. I hate working because I'm actively bad at it.

My first job was at a bank in the suburbs of Chicago, which you might think is an odd place for a sixteen-year-old to work, and I would agree, but my mother's best friend worked there and I've never been above blatant nepotism. Working at a bank when you're sixteen is just like in the movies where the boy next door works at some cute place like a Dairy Queen and gets cute dollops of ice cream on his nose while he's dipping cones in melted chocolate, except instead of a Dairy Queen, it was the accounting department that my mom's friend worked at, and instead of ice cream, it was blotches of charcoal toner from the malfunctioning office printer. Basically the same thing.

It was an old bank, the same one that my mom worked at when she was my age but had to quit because she got knocked up with my brother and chose a life of motherhood instead of a fulfilling career in suburban banking. One of her best friends still oversaw the accounting department, and I politely hinted at a family party that I was finally old enough to legally wear a necktie in public and that perhaps I could use a job that might help pay for my budding necktie collection and that my passion, obviously, was to work in the accounting department of the local branch of my friendly neighborhood bank. Besides, when I was a kid, I used to go to my dad's office and sit in the corner with one of those receipt machines and type numbers into it wildly as it spit out an ever-winding snake of paper containing my meaningless calculations. It made me feel important, because people with receipt machines are important, and it was possibly the only qualification I had to work at an actual financial institution. My mother's friend said she would see what she could do, perhaps there were some menial tasks I could help with during the summer. The next day, I was officially an accounting associate.

I wore a button-down dress shirt tucked into khakis and a necktie that my dad tied around my neck for my first day. My mom took a picture of me in the kitchen before I left that morning, and it looks like one of those pictures that terrorists take of people they've kidnapped, except sadder.

I spent the first year of my life working as an exotic dancer for the local all-male strip club, "Bangers and Ass," where I played the role of "hot football captain who lost his shirt on the way to scoring a touchdown in your end zone." This is the only known photograph of me with a football.

Did I have an actual ginger mullet for the first two years of my life, which flowed in the wind and brushed gently against my rosy cheeks every time I laughed maniacally in the attic where I slept? Absolutely.

The first known picture of me eating cake alone, an activity that would eventually become my most treasured hobby.

Hell yeah, I'm into sports. Played a little in my day. Swung a few bats. Held a few balls. Sniffed a few jockstraps. All that sports stuff.

My Family

Right after this picture w taken, that boat sank, an we only surviv because we were able to use my mother's hair as a flotation device.

I'm only smiling in this photograph because I managed to prevent my mother from applying the green face paint that completed this ensemble but also made me gag like I was deep-throating a Popsicle.

This is a photo of my twin brother, who died of violent static shock after going down this slide one very dry summer day. He touched the metal screw and BAM, exploded into a thousand pieces. We only have a finger to remember him by.

Barney was my ride-or-die sidepiece for, like, three years before I had to break up with him because he started taking up too much space in bed. It was pretty devastating for both of us, but you move on eventually.

As a child of squalor, my only playthings were lawn chairs and empty cardboard boxes, which I fashioned into a house because I wasn't allowed to live inside. My brother and cousin would visit me for the five minutes I was allowed to socialize.

It should come as a surprise to absolutely no one that I chose the most hated character in the Star Wars universe as my Halloween costume. But thassa-me!

Yes, I got all the bitches in kindergarten. And yes, they loved me for my choice of chunky nineties sweaters and show-stopping holiday headwear.

The day I broke my hymen and became a woman.

The exact moment when I realized I would retire at the age of seventeen as the kingpin of my very own Beanie Babies empire.

Our first dog, Frankie, used to sleep inside a pile of blankets in the corner and I used to put my face right up against it and make growling noises. Frankie bit me on the mouth and we had to give him away to a family with smarter children.

My childhood neighbors and I liked to play a game called "Which of us is dressing up for fun and which of us is expressing his inner goal of becoming a gay superstar Clearly, I won.

If you look closely, you can see that I'm wearing skin-colored tights underneath this Steve Irwin look. And if you're wondering, yes, I did trip on a twig and snag those tights almost immediately after this picture was taken.

There comes a time in every young boy's life when he realizes all he wants for Christmas is an original DVD copy of the seminal hit classic *Freaky Friday*, starring Lindsay Lohan and that lady from the yogurt commercials, and, well, I achieved my dreams pretty early in life.

If you scratch this photo and try to sniff it, you might actually catch a whiff of the sheer odor of awkwardness emanating from my freakishly pubescent body on the day of my First Communion, right before I welcomed Jesus inside of my body.

When I walked into the bank, I was directed to the accounting department: down two flights of stairs, along a long, dark hallway, past the mail room, and beyond the flickering light.

My boss was an oversized woman named Shirley, a professional working mom who wore brightly colored blazers with shoulder pads and gaudy jewelry, and screamed when she sneezed, like an actual scream that you scream when someone is stabbing you with a broken wine bottle. Shirley's office, with a window covered in those corporate white blinds, overlooked the accounting department cubicles. From her throne, she could watch all of us labor beneath her.

The cubicles were what you'd expect from a typical bank office: overhead fluorescent lighting, creaky black desk chairs in front of computers that only produced pale green text on black screens, and hideous carpeting to muffle all of our screams.

Out in the open cubicles sat my coworkers, six middle-aged women—Linda, Patricia, Cynthia, Maxine, Deborah, and Janice—all of whom had worked in that very office for longer than I'd been alive, each crazier than the last, perhaps because they'd been trapped together in that very same basement since the bank was built above it forty years earlier.

Shirley led me to my desk, or rather, led me to the desk I'd be sharing with Janice. I was to be, in essence, Janice's protégé. Janice worked only part-time to begin with, and she was slated to leave for a month in the coming weeks, so my job was to learn her tasks so I could perform them while she was away.

It took thirty minutes to discover just how special Janice truly was. She was a small, paper-thin woman, the kind who might blow away in a particularly weak breeze or fall over after a gentle cough. Her eyes looked like they were always asking for your permission, and you just had to be like, "Janice, stop being weird and show me how the copy machine works." She was constantly crumbling with stress. Every minor problem was a cause for major concern. If we ran out of paper clips, it was a category-five shit storm, and Janice was seconds away from bursting into flames.

We sat side by side at her desk, in front of her whirring computer, and she walked me through her day. First, we looked at all the business checks that needed to be signed by two people and made sure they were actually signed by two people in case a local pizza shop co-owner decided to stage a silent coup in the dead of night and stealthily withdraw all the pizza money from the account he shared with his wife.

As we were flicking through the checks, she stopped me and asked, "Do you have kids?"

My sixteen-year-old self found this question surprising. Yes, in her defense, I was wearing a shirt and tie, which might normally make a person look more mature, but not in my case. Putting a shirt and tie on me was a lot like putting a shirt and tie on a baby, which is to say it made the outside observer even more painfully aware of the fact that what they were looking at was a literal baby in a shirt and tie.

"No," I said. "I'm sixteen."

"Oh," Janice said. "Well. My daughter just turned eighteen and she's having her second baby."

"Oh," I said. "Congratulations."

"Yeah," Janice said. "And it's with a different guy this time."

"Oh," I said. "Well, that's . . . nice, I guess."

I should point out that I have absolutely no judgment of Janice's daughter. I mean, hell, she'd gotten two more guys to knock her up than I ever had. Good for her. I hope by now she's had ten other babies with ten other guys and every Christmas she takes a picture with all the kids on Santa's lap and then she mails the picture to all twelve of her babies' daddies with a note that says, "Once you pop, the fun don't stop." It would be adorable, and I'd be happy for her.

Still, though, how is a sixteen-year-old virgin supposed to respond to that information? Especially when it's being provided by a woman I'd met literal seconds before this. But this was my first job, and I wasn't really sure how people were supposed to behave in an office environment. Maybe teen pregnancy was just what grown-ups talked about when they worked.

As the days wore on, it became painfully obvious that I had no idea what I was doing. I was a child playing office with a receipt machine. When it came time for my twenty-minute lunch break, I'd stand outside Shirley's office and wait for her to get off the phone, like a kid waiting for his mom to get out of the bathroom, just so I could ask her for permission to walk down the hallway to the break room and eat the snack I'd brought from home. I thought I wasn't allowed to leave the room without her express permission. Some days, I'd spend longer than twenty minutes just waiting to get her attention.

To give you a full picture of just how bad I was at this job, and how ridiculous it was to let a sixteen-year-old boy be in charge of money that didn't come with a board game, I fucked up one particularly important task.

One of my jobs was to process something called fraud reports. To this day, I don't entirely understand what those fraud reports were, but they sounded important. Fraud is a bad word in general, and it's a particularly bad word at a bank where, ya know, people keep their money and jewels. A fraud report, I assume, was something that required a great deal of care. From what I remember, it was a rundown of all sorts of flagged activity, like unusual withdrawals or transfers or weird signatures, like when your credit card company calls you and asks if it's really you that's been spending one hundred and fifty dollars a day at the dildo emporium in Queens, and you have to explain that yes, it's perfectly acceptable for a grown man to visit the dildo emporium at eleven in the morning on a Tuesday, as you've explained before, so please stop calling this number because the emporium charges are going to continue.

I worked at the central branch of the bank, and my fraud report task was to break down each day's accounts by branch and fax out a copy of the relevant information to the corresponding locations. Essentially, a little message to say, "Hey, one of your clients is maybe getting robbed, so be on the look-out for that." Each day, I would make a small pile for each branch—I was nothing if not an organized gay—and, one by one, carry the stacks to the fax machine, because yes, we used fax machines, this was the 2000s and fax machines were the height of telecommunications technology, and I'd send each stack on its merry little way.

For the children who may be unfamiliar, a fax machine was the monstrous bastard child of a phone, a printer, a scanner, a calculator, and the devil, and to wield power over it, one had to smear the blood of one's firstborn son at the machine's feet, so as to appease the beast within. I believe, to this day, that no person on earth has ever truly learned all the secrets of a fax machine. Really, you just push a bunch of buttons in rapid succession, and then jam your thumb onto a giant green switch, and pray to God that whatever you're trying to send happens to make its way to the other side. It's about 5 percent technology, 95 percent voodoo magic.

I, however, prided myself on my fax machine mastery. Not to be crude, but I made that fax machine my bitch. I owned that shit. Every day, I walked over to that machine, and typed each number like I was slicing open the sternum of a dying patient so I could imbue her with a new beating heart that I'd grown myself from a petri dish. The machine was my instrument, and faxing was my beautiful music.

I was so confident in my work that, after every session, I would take each branch's stack of fraud reports to the shredder and dump them in, the crunching of the paper acting as my final confirmation of mastery over my domain.

It wasn't until one day some weeks into my accounting career that I noticed, as I was confidently strumming numbers into the fax machine's dial pad, that a tiny symbol on the document feeder showed a little piece of paper whose corner was folded to show lines of text on the opposite side—a symbol, in other words, to suggest that documents were to be inserted *text side down*. I had not been inserting my documents *text side down*. I had been inserting my documents *text side up*, which meant that each day, when I'd delicately organized my fraud report piles, carried them one by one to the fax machine, placed them finely into the document feeder, effortlessly typed the numbers into the dial pad, and listened seductively as the music of each digit's tone rang in my ear and the machine buzzed to life, slurping up my papers and spitting them out, emitting a final climactic beep to indicate the transaction was complete, throughout all this time, I'd been faxing *the blank side of the paper out into the world and then shredding the originals*. Every day, measly accounting associates in local bank branches around the greater Chicagoland area were wondering why in the hell their fax machines were buzzing awake in the middle of the day to spit out blank stacks of paper, and also why they hadn't been receiving any fresh fraud reports lately and if perhaps we'd simply eradicated fraud altogether but somehow inherited a fax machine virus. I'd been sowing silent chaos for weeks, and I had no idea.

Because I was never entirely sure how important those fraud reports were, I don't know how much damage I caused by allowing some six weeks of fraud to go uninvestigated, but I should point out for posterity that the bank in question is no longer in business, and I can't say that I am solely or even partially responsible for that fact, but I also can't say that I'm not.

For the sake of owning up to my faults and placing responsibility where it belongs, I'd like to say that I absolutely and completely blame Janice for this mistake. It's obviously *possible* that she showed me how to use the fax machine correctly on day one, but let's be real, she probably didn't. And for that, Janice can never be forgiven. Obviously she should've taken greater care to show a young, helpless child like myself that you have to place your stack of precious documents in the fax machine one way or they may never be seen by a person in the world ever again.

And while we're accepting blame, I'd also like to blame literally every other person in that office for being such a distraction. Maybe I would've faxed those documents correctly had it not been for Cynthia, who got up every ten minutes to smoke a cigarette and on more than one occasion, if my nose was right, drink from a flask of vodka she kept in her blazer pocket. Or for Patricia, who spoke rapid, angry Spanish into her desk phone for hours on end. Or for Deborah, who went to the movie theater with her boyfriend every Friday to see literally every movie released that week, only to come in on Monday and recount each plot in its entirety with absolutely no regard for spoilers. Or, worst of all, were it not for Janice and her aura of darkness.

I don't want to discredit the obvious stress she was under as a working woman responsible for two grandchildren, but as my days as a full-blown accounting associate continued, so did Janice's days as the epitome of melancholia.

On one afternoon, the girls and I were talking about vacations we'd been on, presumably to try visualizing some form of escape from the hell we were then laboring under. Maxine had recently been to Denver with her new husband. I was getting ready to go to Michigan with my family. Deborah couldn't take vacations because she'd miss that week's newest movies and it would throw off her whole schedule. It was a lovely conversation.

And then, out of nowhere, Janice says, "Well, we like to go camping. But the last time we went, our dog committed suicide."

There was silence before someone said, "Wait. What?"

Yes, Janice explained, they'd been camping recently and had set up one of those elevated tents, the kind that ties to a few different tree trunks and hangs a couple feet above the ground to make the tent less accessible to bears or other woodland menaces, and when they stepped away, their dog managed to nuzzle the tent flap open and jump out. But he was still wearing his leash and he never made it to the ground.

Now, if your mouth is hanging open, you are not alone. We all sat in silence trying to process what she'd just said, entirely unprompted. Classic Janice.

"Jesus, Janice!" I said. "That's awful." Because that's the only thing you can say to that kind of thing. Even though what you really wanna say is, "I don't blame him. I would've done the same."

That conversation trailed off into nothing.

But that was hardly the height of Janice's melodrama.

There was a handful of weeks where Janice left on grand-maternity leave, and I took over her tasks full-time. It was a perfectly fine month, despite the fraud report mess (which, by the way, nobody ever noticed, and you know I kept that shit to myself). I was free to wreak havoc entirely on my own. And yes, in case you're wondering, I *did* have access to everybody's account information—again, no bank should have given a sixteen-year-old this level of clearance—and yes, I *did* look up all of my friends' bank accounts. *For business.*

When Janice finally returned, rather than having her resume the duties she'd been responsible for forever and that I had surreptitiously taken over, Shirley relegated her to a series of menial secretarial tasks that needed dedicated work.

Now, far be it from me to point out that it should've been the sixteen-year-old pipsqueak who got demoted to bitch work, and not the desolate woman who had worked there for years, but it was Shirley's decree, and she was bigger and louder than all of us, so we did what she said. It also didn't help that it was painfully obvious that I'd only gotten this job because my mother's friend ran the whole place, that I was only a pimply interloper who had come into Janice's space and declared it my own. But I do as I'm told.

Here was Janice's task. Sometimes, people get sued. Sometimes they get sued because of money stuff. It's very complicated, and I would explain it to you, but honestly you wouldn't understand. Just trust me on this. Sometimes, when people get sued because of money stuff, they have to produce a bunch of documents, like bank statements and cashed checks and pictures of receipts from the dildo emporium, and it's up to the bank to print all that shit out, except maybe the dildo receipts, but all the rest of it for sure. And this particular summer, there was a case that required every document from one account for basically the past thirty years. Which sounds like a perfectly easy task until you remember that Al Gore didn't invent the Internet until 1996, and almost all of those documents weren't on a computer. Instead, images of all of those checks were on tiny rolls of Kodak film that had to be inserted into a tiny machine and scrolled through individually, like a giant version of one of those ghastly red View-Master toys from the 1970s that you held up to your face and clicked through to see pictures of Bambi's mom getting shot.

The Kodak machine was kept in a dank, windowless closet

in a corner of the basement, and whoever was on printing duty (Janice, God bless her feeble soul) had to sit in a tiny chair in front of the film machine and individually turn through and print thousands of checks, one at a time, hour by hour, for days on end. In retrospect, I'm convinced that the film machine was not actually designed by Kodak for printing images, but created as some type of governmental experiment on mind control and torture, devised to reduce its users to their basest forms. By intention, I think, they designed the machine to run out of toner after every twenty-five pages, and you'd have to turn the whole damn thing around, take out its toner feed bag, shake it like you were seasoning a chicken breast, and put it back in the machine in the hopes that your shakes had reinvigorated its will to cooperate. But of course, each time you retrieved the toner bag, the machine would cough out a plume of thick black smoke that would settle on your hands and face and pants and lungs, because the room was the size of a closed oven and there was nowhere you could move to escape the inky cloud. You would emerge from printing duty like a coal miner returning from the shaft. It was the office equivalent of solitary confinement.

It took approximately three days for Janice to break entirely. Before noon on the third day, the machine had already jammed ten times, she'd shaken the toner bag a dozen times more, and smashed the machine to within an inch of its life, and finally, she came stumbling from the room wailing in distress, absolutely covered in charcoal toner dust, her sobs creating clear streaks of tears through the black soot on her cheeks, her hair a nest of ink and blood and tears, her body a shriveled shell of its already shriveled former self, stained, soiled, and defeated.

We all surrounded her like a dog that had just been rescued from a well, patting her on the back and offering her water and food from our hands. Of course, there was nothing else I could do. I volunteered to take Janice's place, but Shirley was sending her home to recuperate, and the regular work needed to be done.

The next day, Janice returned and Shirley relegated her to some other menial task in a different closet with a different machine folding papers that needed to be stuffed into envelopes, and it took an hour before Janice came sobbing around the corner yet again, and Shirley had to be like, "Goddammit, Janice, get your shit together," and she got sent home another time and we all kind of silently bowed our heads.

The rest of that summer didn't get much better. You may be wondering what happened to Janice, and the truth is, I have no idea. I think her only relief was that I eventually went back to school and quit working. I can only assume she died halfway through Deborah's retelling of *Avatar*, but nobody can be sure.

But there are three lessons I'd like to point out from this summer as an accounting associate. First, having an office job is basically like working in a coal mine, so we need to stop acting like those are two completely different things, because my lungs are still covered in toner (yes, I had to finish the job that Janice couldn't). Two, we cannot send our nation's Janices to the inevitable war against the robots, because we will fail. And three, never trust a child with your community's finances unless you want an entire banking institution to crumble. You've been warned.

. . .

Of course, I'd like to think that working at that bank prepared me for life aboveground, but I left that office less equipped for the world than before.

The next summer, I got a job as a cashier at a department store, and I won't tell you what department store that was, but I will tell you that this particular department store has way too many fucking coupons. And coupons are a scam, unless you're one of those people on one of those extreme couponing shows, which doesn't prove anything except that some people in Middle America have too much time on their hands and also too much room in their houses for five hundred excess packages of paper towels.

Here's the thing that you learn almost immediately when you work in retail: the customer is absolutely never right. When you get a job at this particular department store, they make you watch an orientation video in a little room behind one of those doors that says "Employees Only," and the video that tells you things like "don't sexually harass your coworker Brenda" and also "the customer is always right," except the problem is, only one of those things is actually true. It's actually dangerous to be teaching these two things together when one of them is so obviously a lie, because it casts doubt on the whole damn production. We'd all be better off if the presentation just said, "Listen. Don't sexually harass Brenda and also, the guy who wants 15 percent off that kitchen mixer he found in the sale bin can go fuck himself because it was never in the sale bin and he knows it."

Retail workers experience the worst of America every single day, and most of the time, we don't even let them sit while they do it. You just have to stand there behind a cash register for hours while people yell at you, because that's what retail is: getting yelled at. You'd think, perhaps, that as a working professional I'd have been better at dealing with people, but considering the only other job I'd had was spent working in an office underground, my people skills were generally lacking, and yes, I got yelled at a whole bunch.

There was a man who yelled at me because I refused to accept a one-hundred-dollar bill so he could take a shirt that he hadn't yet purchased out to his car and compare it to a pair of pants he'd bought somewhere else, which theoretically makes sense, since the shirt was probably worth only six dollars to begin with, but still! You can't just go around letting people leave the store with stuff they didn't pay for! I kindly explained that he could purchase the shirt and return it if it didn't work out, but he definitely couldn't just walk out of the store with it, so he bought it and brought it back to return it and then I was like, "Sir, you have to take this to customer service because I can't process your return here," and then he turned the kind of red that you only see on chickens' dangly things and he started cursing at me, and honestly, I probably would've cursed at me, too, but those are the rules.

There was a guy who tried purchasing a candle that someone had left on the shelf from another store (because it was truly an ugly candle and, I assume, they happened to come to their senses and abandon it then and there). I tried to explain that there was no way I could sell this man the candle because it wasn't ours to sell (honestly, he could've just taken it), but he insisted on paying for it and refused to leave until I could tell him the price.

There was a woman who asked me where the exercise equipment was, and I pointed her to the opposite corner of the store, only for her to return twenty minutes later to scream that she'd said "exercise clothes," which happened to be directly behind where I was standing all along.

There was a group of teenagers who tried to buy a pair of pants with a bunch of jewelry stuffed in the pockets, and when I pulled it out, they yelled at me for trying to accuse them of youthful thievery.

There was a woman who yelled at me because I refused to accept her coupon because it had expired, and normally we were supposed to accept expired coupons, but her coupon had expired eight years earlier and there are literally new coupons every week. I mean, c'mon. Put in some basic effort, lady.

And finally there was the woman who accused me of trying to ruin her credit score by asking her to sign up for a store credit card, even though all I was doing was trying to save her 15 percent.

But here's where I need to pause and say, sometimes, the customer has a point. I'm not saying they're right. I'm just saying, sometimes they have a point.

I hate when cashiers ask me to sign up for a store credit card. Sure, you save 15 percent now, but then you miss one payment and they charge you a bajillion dollars in interest fees and I already recklessly spend enough money without my money costing me even more money, so I'd rather we just avoid that whole mess and I pay with normal money like Jesus intended when he invented department stores in the first place. But of course "no" is never an acceptable answer when 15 percent off your entire purchase is at stake, and there's an inevitable back-and-forth that always ends with the cashier casting judgment on you for refusing their kind and charitable attempt to save you seven dollars off a pair of pants that you'll only wear for a month.

Having been on the other side of that transaction, though, I can say that it's not any better for the cashier either, especially if you're as terrible at salesmanship as I am. After all, I was hired as a cashier, not a salesperson. My job was to swipe your poor fashion choices over a laser inside a countertop and then tell you how much money you were shitting away. Nothing in my job description called for trying to trick people who shouldn't have credit cards into signing up for a fucking credit card. Trying to sell people credit cards felt dirty. The first trick: when a customer is ready to check out, ask them, "Will this be going on your store card today?" If they say yes, great, we've already got 'em. If they say no, then you've got yourself a brand-new target. Congratulations, you're halfway to being a sleazy credit-card salesman.

Of course, as dirty as it is, there's a little thing called incentives, and in this case, every time I got someone to fill out an application ("It only takes two minutes! I just need your social security number, a driver's license, and a urine sample, but the bathroom is right there!"), I'd get two whole dollars. And sure, it seemed like a lot of begging for only two dollars, but when you make eight dollars an hour, an extra two dollars every hour is nothing to piss at. Plus, every time you scored an application, you got to pick up the store intercom phone and announce "Code 4-7," which was a signal to all the other store employees that you'd gotten a credit card application and were therefore better than them. Besides, you were helping the less fortunate by saving them 15 percent off their entire purchase!

But mixing together competition, credit scores, and adolescent stupidity isn't the greatest idea in the world. Before long, I got into a daily "Code 4-7" battle with Rose, the jewelry counter cashier who nabbed a few applicants every hour. I couldn't lose to an old woman hawking 15 percent off tawdry bracelets under the jewelry-counter lights.

The most common refrain from customers was "I don't think I'd get approved," which is a perfectly normal and responsible thing to say. If you know your credit score is bad, trying to sign up for a new credit card is probably not the greatest idea. But I found out that we could still give customers the 15 percent discount even if their application wasn't approved. Which seems like a terrible business decision, but I didn't question it. After I found that out, I'd start telling customers, "Look. It doesn't hurt to fill out an application. Even if you don't get approved, you'll still get 15 percent off!"

In my defense, I was seventeen, I had never had a credit card, and I didn't know what the fuck a credit score actually was. To be perfectly honest, I'm still not even sure what a credit score is, and I have no idea what makes it go up or down, besides making monthly sacrifices at the tomb of J. P. Morgan. So seventeen-year-old me, in those tight khakis and that ill-fitting black polo shirt, had no clue I was doing a bad thing, that I was exploiting the terrible financial choices of unsuspecting consumers. I just wanted two extra dollars and the satisfaction of hearing my voice reverberate throughout the store over Jewelry Counter Rose's cries.

It was all fun and games until one day, when Rose was on a particularly successful streak, I got desperate and pressed a woman who I should've known was a clear and obvious "no" if she was *absolutely sure* she didn't want to save 15 percent off her gorgeous selection of capri pants and crop tops ("Even if you don't qualify, you'll still get the discount off these amazing looks!") and she snapped and launched into a long (and not at all unwarranted) tirade on why corporations were ruining the middle class, and at some point in her screams, I'm pretty sure she predicted the 2008 financial crisis, but I wasn't entirely sure because I was crying at the time.

After that incident—and a not-so-gentle reminder from my boss that the point of offering discounts was to try to get *approved* applications so we could screw people for *months* and not just one day—I eased off my grind and allowed Rose to take it away. I figured I'd let her have this. Cosmically speaking, letting Rose get ahead was my way of making up for Janice. Even though that clearly wasn't the case.

. . .

My third and final job as a struggling adolescent (before I graduated college and became a struggling adult) was a desk job at the law school of my undergraduate alma mater. I thought, for a few terrifying months, that perhaps I'd graduate and go to law school. Nothing in my professional history suggested this was a good idea, but I was an asshole and I liked money, so I figured I might be able to give it a shot. Working at a law school would put me right where the action was.

I got an interview and wore my finest shirt and tie, tucked into my finest khakis. It was June, the beginning of the height of summer in Chicago, and ninety degrees outside. I was living at home in the suburbs that summer, and the law school was downtown, right down the street from the famous Chicago water tower, but a full train ride and bus ride away from where I was.

I was not used to taking trains, especially not commuter trains. The only train I'd ever *really* taken was the train at the zoo that takes you around to all the different animals so you don't have to walk. Commuter trains are way too intense, mostly because the same people ride them every single morning. That's the suburban routine, a manifestation of the American dream. You live in a nice family house in the suburbs, and every morning, you kiss your children goodbye, pour a nice big travel mug of coffee, get on a train, and ride it to your fancy office in the city. It's literally the same people you're traveling with every morning. They all stand in the same spot on the train platform so they can hop on the same car and get to the same seat, where they read the same newspaper over and over every day until they die. It's terrifying to witness. One morning that summer, on my birthday no less, my mom called me from home to wish me a happy birthday because she'd been asleep when I left. She barely made it to the second stanza before the woman behind me violently tapped me on the shoulder to scold me for taking a phone call on the "quiet car." I was quiet car shamed! On my own birthday! Commuter trains are intense.

Of course, the day of my interview was my first day taking the train. I waited on the platform with my messenger bag around my shoulder and across my chest like a true budding cosmopolitan professional. I was already nervous. There was a lot going on at the train platform. A man with a clipboard was going around asking for signatures to support his candidacy for neighborhood council, and I had to tell him no three times before he'd leave me alone. It was all very overstimulating. As the train came into view, though, I started to panic. What if I was on the wrong side of the tracks? What if I got on this train and it took me in the wrong direction? Before I had a chance to ask any of my fellow passengers, the train had arrived, the doors were opening, a conductor was yelling "all aboard," and I was freaking out. So I stepped onto the train, one foot still on the platform, and tried asking the first person I could find if this was heading into Chicago, but she hesitated, and so did I, and the door started closing while I was still partially on the platform. I managed to get my second foot into the train before the door shut entirely, but my messenger bag, that holy symbol of young budding professionalism, got caught by the doors and trapped outside of the train, still wrapped around my torso, pinning me to the inside of the door with the strap tight against my chest like a car seat belt when you slam on the brakes. It was just slack enough for me to wriggle myself out of it, but the bag was still trapped outside of the doors, dangling out there like a loose button. I tried desperately to pry the doors open, but either I was too weak or they were too strong, because they didn't budge. There was an emergency brake, but I'm terrible at deciding what amounts to an emergency, most of all when I'm in the middle of an emergency, and I didn't pull it. I could do nothing but bang on the doors in exasperation and hope there'd be no tight tunnels between this station and the next.

Luckily, just as hope seemed all but lost and I'd kissed all of my prized belongings away, including, most important, my stack of laminated résumés and, less important, my six-year-old laptop computer, a man on the platform—the man with the clipboard no less, at whom I'd scoffed minutes earlier—noticed my bag, and my wildly frightened face in the window, and he started waving his arms wildly at the conductor, and another person closer to the front of the train started waving *their* arms, and together they managed to get his attention. And just as the train was getting ready to lurch forward, it calmed to a halt and the doors opened.

I'm already prone to sweating, but I'm especially prone to sweating in humid summer heat, and I'm *especially* prone to sweating when I just got pinned against a train door. When I was in high school, I'd apply two coats of clinical-strength deodorant every morning before school and two again after gym class, and every morning, I'd wear an extra T-shirt underneath my clothes as a sort of buffer cloth to catch the excess moisture. There's a paradox in a buffer sweat shirt, considering that the extra sweat-catching layer adds another piece of cloth to trap heat, but I did what had to be done to minimize the amount of visible leakage.

When I finally made it downtown, took a bus, and got off at the stop closest to the law school, some four blocks away from the building I was interviewing in, I walked through the humid Chicago heat in blaring sunlight. By the time I reached the building, I'd already sweat through the entirety of my buffer shirt and it was starting to leak through the outer layers. I flicked some water on my face from a water fountain on the first floor and stood with my legs and arms spread apart for a few minutes in an attempt to will away as much of the moisture as I could. But I was already running late.

And to make matters even fucking worse, there was no elevator and the office was on the fourth fucking floor. That's the thing about these old university buildings. They tell you, "Oh, we're such a great university, we've been teaching law to smart-asses since 1851, but also, our buildings were built before elevators existed so have fun walking up three thousand steps in the blistering heat because also air conditioners didn't exist when this building was built either."

When I made it up those four flights of stairs, my legs were shaking, my chest was heaving, and my body was spraying sweat clear across the room every time I turned my head. Call it a combination of nerves, stress, and utter weakness, but I was having some kind of attack, possibly of the heart variety or more likely the panic variety, and it wasn't pretty.

Jackie, the head of the department I was interviewing for, found me leaning against the wall trying to catch my breath, and offered me a towel—not just a tissue, but a *towel*—and I said, "No thank you, I brought my own towel," and eventually we went into her office, and I sat in front of a fan, and everything went just wonderfully after that.

I got the job, obviously—Jackie was no idiot—but I did have to walk up those stairs every morning, and it took a full two months before my entire body stopped convulsing after the entire process. Although the actual office wasn't any better than the staircase. The only air-conditioning in the reception room where I worked was a spitting window unit that took approximately seventeen hours to start breathing. My first week, there was a wasp nest outside the window, so we couldn't even open it for relief. And somehow, the wasps would find their way in, and obviously, because I was the biggest and youngest and manliest (i.e., the only man), it was my responsibility to kill them.

But I worked in that shitty jungle office for three entire summers. And it wasn't in a basement. And there were no goddamn customers. So I'd say I'd moved sufficiently far up in life.

ON MY TROUBLED HISTORY WITH FASHION

I have no idea what to wear. And I don't mean right now, because right now I'm wearing gym shorts, socks, and a T-shirt, and I'm perfectly comfortable with rocking this whole look, but eventually, I'm gonna have to get out of bed, and I'll have to put on something that is generally acceptable to wear in public. And I have no idea what to wear.

Everybody expects gays to have a sense of style, but I blame the ladies on *Queer Eye for the Straight Guy* and the preppy couple from *Glee* for that one. Thanks to them, society expects me to flawlessly execute a fitted blazer, bow tie, suspenders, skinny pants, and a thong at any given moment, and I can barely put on two of the same socks in the morning, let alone an on-theme ensemble.

For one, being fat kinda hinders one's ability to pull off a good look. And yes, I know, there's a whole bunch of blogs for plus-sized fashion for women *and* men, and they all say I just have to close my eyes and believe in myself and also maybe wear vertical stripes, but the truth is, when the mannequin at J.Crew has a rippling six-pack, it's kinda hard to muster the confidence to rock the same getup.

Walking into a dressing room always goes a little something like this:

I enter, confident, with an armful of button-down shirts and blue jeans. I take off my current clothes and pile them in a heap in the corner. I start with a shirt, because that should be the easy thing to do, and also I don't have to take off my undershirt for this and can spare myself my own grotesque reflection, but of course, I can only button the first few buttons before things start to strain and I can hear the tiny sweatshop children who sewed these seams together start to cry. I give up on the entire pile of shirts, because if one doesn't fit, they all probably don't fit, and nothing matters anymore. I start putting on a pair of pants in the same size I bought my last pants in only a few months earlier, but my bulbous calves barely fit past the part that should hold my entire thigh. I'm hopping on one foot and grasping at the curtains, because that's what dressing rooms are these days, curtains instead of walls so you have nothing solid to hold on to when you need to lean against something and cry. At this point, I'm stuck inside the pants, my entire leg is sweating from ankle to crotch, my back is dripping, and my glasses are falling from my face. I can hear the sales associate shuffling uncomfortably on the other side of the curtain, because that's the thing about curtains instead of doors, they don't really muffle your screams, especially since they always leave a gap sizable enough for a little girl standing nearby to witness you bouncing haplessly in your underwear.

"Is everything OK in there?" the sales associate is asking. "Do you need any help?" Which is not a question you want someone asking when you're trying on pants. "NO, I GOT IT," I shout back at her. "YOUR CLOTHES ARE JUST THE DEVIL." And then I finally break free, ripping the pants at the seam and coughing as loud as I can to cover the sound of the fabric tearing in distress. When I finally open the curtain and step outside, back in the potato sack I walked in wearing, I look like I've just taken a shower, and the sales associate asks if I'd like to sit down for a minute and drink a bottle of water, or perhaps dab myself with a beach towel. I politely decline, and before they have a chance to convince me that I didn't try squeezing hard enough, I run out of the store, knocking down a stack of T-shirts on the way out.

It should go without saying that none of this is hypothetical. Which is why I not only avoid dressing rooms, but avoid purchasing new clothes altogether.

Besides, when you're a little chunky, and you've always been a little chunky, you tend not to fall in love with any one item of clothing, because chances are, you won't fit into it in a few months anyway. (Except, of course, shoes, although there are those moments in life when you discover you've somehow gotten too fat for those, too, and you'll want to die more than ever. I mean, really? How much weight do you have to gain to *get too fat for your shoes?*)

Worst of all, clothes are expensive as fuck. Especially good clothes that are flattering and look nice and don't immediately fall apart the second you put them on. Why spend eighty dollars on a quality shirt when that same money could buy four and a half chicken-alfredo dinners with a side of garlic knots from the Olive Garden? Looking like shit is just economical.

All the same, there comes a time in every young gay's life when he must contend with the clothes on his back, and I've made my choices. I've finally settled on a uniform of plaid button-downs, blue jeans, and sneakers—a simple outfit that looks like I've put in at least minimal effort without having to think about it. But it took years to perfect this image, and plenty of trial and error (mostly error) to get the perfect look. I present to you: fashion through the ages, or my troubled history with clothing.

THE ATHLETICA AGE: Like all homosexual children, I was a victim of circumstances, and by circumstances, I mean my parents' terrible choices. Dissatisfied to wallow in their own shoulder-padded misery alone, they imprisoned me in all manner of sports-themed onesies, overalls, and jumpers, full of baseballs, footballs, and tennis rackets, striped to look like a referee or, God forbid, an actual athlete, all before I could even walk or speak. I don't mean to overexaggerate, but this, plain and simple, was textbook heterosexual indoctrination, and I blame it for everything wrong in my childhood, including the brief stint I spent in basketball camp, where I was forced to learn such propaganda terms as "free throw," "layup," and "dribble." Even worse, almost every portrait of me from the first year of my life is staged with an actual, real-life football that they made me touch, cuddle, and smile beside. It was horrifying.

And I know some of you are thinking, "THEY'RE BABY CLOTHES! THEY'RE CUTE! WHAT DO YOU WANT INSTEAD? GENDERLESS PIL-LOW SACKS WITH LIMB HOLES?" And the answer is yes. I would prefer genderless pillow sacks with limb holes. Perhaps babies of the future will be spared the indignity of having to look back and see their infant selves cradling sports equipment.

THE PINK AGE: When I was old enough to dress myself, my favorite item of clothing became a bright pink T-shirt, which the manlier members of my family con-sidered suspicious. This was the nineties, after all, when liking pink things as a young boy was still considered a misdemeanor in most states. But I loved pink—all the best things in life were pink: Kirby the Nintendo blob, bubble gum, donut frosting, piggy banks, cotton candy, and the only flavor of Starburst that actually matters. That shirt represented my entire worldview before soci-ety tore me down.

Of course, that shirt soon got buried beneath the piles and piles of hand-me-downs my mother trans-ferred from my brother's closet to mine. We were a fru-gal family, and my parents never wasted an opportunity to save a penny, especially if it meant embarrassing my brother or me. Case in point: on more than one occa-sion, my mother forced me to snatch a piece of old fur-niture from a neighbor's garbage. We'd be driving home from school and she'd spot some old desk or flea-ridden armchair and demand that I run out and grab it. "You're the one who wants it," I'd yell. "You get it!" But I was small and weak, and she was the boss, and inevitably, I'd be pilfering from the trash while she kept the getaway car running two driveways ahead. The same general philosophy applied to clothes: you get what you get, especially if it comes from the trash. And sure, maybe it wasn't from the literal trash, maybe it was just from my brother's collection of old shit, but still. My brother was always taller and ganglier than me, so I spent most of my grade-school years in chunky sweaters and loose jeans that were always just a bit off, constantly reminded that clothing was something that wore *me*, rather than the other way around.

THE AMERICANA AGE: One day, when I was finally becoming old enough to care, my mother came home with a sackful of T-shirts she'd found on sale at Kohl's and plopped them on the kitchen table. Kohl's being Kohl's, they'd cost only a couple of dollars each, and she bought every design they had on the shelf, nearly twenty in total, which would last me the entire year. Yes, this is all well and good, and children in starving countries would be blessed to have parents who brought them home sackfuls of T-shirts they'd bought on sale from Kohl's. But here's the thing. This particular sale happened to be in honor of the Fourth of July, so every shirt in my mother's bountiful Kohl's sack was a deep shade of either red, white, or blue, all with gaudy American decals on the front—a majestic eagle, an American flag, or some other horrific flourish. And sure, this was midwestern suburbia, where patriotism was plentiful. But there's a limit to the amount of Americana a thirteen-year-old can display in public before it starts to look like he's on some type of special government scholarship that requires a constant display of fealty to the state. Fortunately, with puberty's ascendance, my sweat glands went into overdrive and nearly disintegrated all the armpits. So the joke, really, was on Kohl's and their cheap T-shirts.

THE CARGO JORTS AGE: I remain convinced that cargo shorts are one of the least flattering, most unbearable items of clothing ever invented. I mean, surely there are better places to keep your fish hooks and tackle gear than a lower thigh pocket. Like a fishing box. Or a garbage can. The point is, cargo shorts are basically just the straight man's response to purses. Women carry everything they need in a purse, but because masculinity says your penis is too small if you carry your stuff in a bag, some man in medieval times was like, "How about we just build purses right onto these shorts?" And now we have cargo shorts. And the world is terrible because of them.

Of course, I didn't know this until I found the light some years later in life. And so, I spent most of my high school years on the wrong side of history, wearing cargo shorts almost daily. And not just any cargo shorts. *Jean* cargo shorts. Cargo *jorts*. And what did I keep in them? Definitely not my dignity.

I'm proud to say those cargo jorts have been burned

alongside everything I ever attempted to buy from Abercrombie & Fitch. I hope they're burning in hell.

THE RALPH LAUREN AGE: When I started college, I still had little idea of what constituted acceptable fashion, but at the age of eighteen—far later than some of my more astute, non-cargo-jort-wearing classmates—I finally started to realize that clothes weren't just functional. In fact, clothes were the opposite of functional. They existed only to make you uncomfortable and to signal to the world that you had money or taste, or that you cared enough to make people think you had either. Oblivious to fashion beyond what I saw directly before me, I did the best I could and mimicked college bro culture: I replaced all of my T-shirts with Ralph Lauren polos, my cargo jorts with pocketless khaki shorts, and my raggedy sneakers with boat shoes. I'm not proud of this time in my life. Mostly because it was the first time I had to take full ownership and responsibility for what I put on my body. Honestly, if I had come across me in 2008, I would've happily drowned myself in a lake and left the boat shoes to drift away as a symbol of the sins I committed that year. It was a dark time.

THE PURPLE UNDERWEAR AGE: When I finally came out in my later college years, I hadn't brought any fashion knowledge out with me. But I was determined to show my pride in my own little way. I was interning in Chicago, and on my lunch break, I would wander over to Macy's and browse the underwear aisle, finally deciding to buy a flashy pair of purple undies with white trim that cost me something like fifty dollars because for some reason, something that grazes your butthole all day costs an entire fifty dollars when it's a fancy color. But I was a newly minted gay, and owning a pair of purple underwear felt like an appropriate first step toward my new life as a homosexual. Of course, the underwear didn't come close to fitting my enormous thighs; it was like trying to fit a rubber band around a pork roast. But still, that underwear represented my new foray into the fashion world, one where I made choices for me, even if they cut off all circulation to my lower extremities.

THE PLAID AGE: You would think I'd feel pressure, living in New York City, to care more about my fashion choices, but honestly, I feel like I'm doing everybody here a favor. How else would you spot the *GQ* models of the world if you didn't have a mangy schlub like me to compare them to? You're welcome, David Beckham. Without me, nobody would know how hot and well dressed you are. And I'm perfectly fine with that. Because I don't really have to look at me.

That being said, I have finally landed on what I consider a basic daily costume, a look that's normally reserved for divorced dads but somehow works for me. It's comforting not to think about what I wear every day. All I have to do is pick a shirt from the pile on the ground and hope that the Starbucks barista doesn't notice the multiple yogurt stains on the front before I return to my apartment, take the shirt off, and toss it back onto the pile. It's a system that works. And it only took me three decades to figure out.

ON BEING IN THE CLOSET, OR WHY YOU SHOULD NEVER FALL IN LOVE WITH YOUR STRAIGHT BEST FRIEND

I discovered I was gay like most young boys in America: by dry-heaving through the men's underwear aisle at JCPenney. That's right, conservatives. Capitalism made me gay. If the ad executives at Hanes weren't so worried about selling insecure guys tighty whities by modeling them on oiled, headless hunks, then maybe I'd be married to someone named Beth right now and we'd have two and a half children in Bible school and also Mitt Romney would be president. But you just had to go and show my impressionable, pubescent brain ten-foot-tall posters of bare abs and vague, shapeless bulges, and now I'm a full-blown homosexual who reads the *New Yorker* and drinks iced green tea. You have nobody but yourselves to blame. Though, to be fair, it was the nineties, and men's underwear back then covered the belly button and most of the nipple. But the important thing here is that my brain took the signal and raised the rainbow flags.

I should clarify, of course, for the Texans reading this, that an underwear ad did not actually turn me gay. Nothing can *turn* you gay, no matter what those TV preachers say, not even the seductive stare of an amorphous penis on a package of boxer briefs. I was just plain old born gay, probably because my mother watched too many daytime soap operas while she was pregnant with me, and then, bit by bit, the gayness grew inside me until it finally started seeping from my glands sometime in the late 2000s.

I never had the "AHA" moment you hear about in more dramatic gay people's books, where I'm awkwardly unclasping some poor girl's bra and then, like a bolt of lightning hitting the gay part of the brain, I suddenly realize I'd rather be in a bathhouse with Ryan Gosling. I mean, sure, I've had moments like that. Everybody has moments like that. You can't watch *The Notebook* and *not* have involuntary sexual visions of Ryan Gosling dropping soap in a gym shower. It's part of life. But a thought like that was never the epiphany for me, because there never was some Big Moment of Gay Clarity. It was more like a thousand tiny "MM-HMM" moments that piled up to confirm a nagging suspicion, a buried inkling that I was craving a different cut of beef.

When I was ten, I had my first real hunch when I discovered my brother's poorly hidden adult magazines for heterosexuals. (Apologies to my brother, if he's reading this, but I found your straight porn. You should've gotten a lockbox or something that tripped a silent alarm.) This was before we had a computer, of course, which means he had no choice but to buy disgusting nudie magazines instead of digital porn, and I had no choice but to spend my free time rifling under his mattress instead of, I don't know, doing whatever kids do on the Internet these days (Buy meth?). I remember turning those crinkly pages like a scientist looking through lab samples, taking in those appallingly hairy pictures and running them against a mental database of things that triggered an exciting emotional response. Nothing. When I got to the last page, I remember thinking, out loud, with a clarity I'd never experienced before, "Where the fuck are all the dicks?" It felt like a gross oversight on the part of such an esteemed publication to just forget to feature a whole half of the population. Even then my brain knew one basic fact: everything is better with more penis.

Of course, that was only a hunch. I assumed everybody came to this conclusion at the end of their straight porn perusal. A few years later, I got full confirmation while searching online for posters to hang on my bedroom wall. This was a big moment in its own right, since I was finally replacing one of the many bedroom themes I'd had through adolescence (first "Pokémon," then "Nautica," then "Rainforest Cafe"). I was ready for the more sophisticated, undefined aesthetic of a trendy college dorm, like the kids on *Boy Meets World*. This was the 2000s after all, I'd survived Y2K, and it was time to enhance my bedroom game with a few posters that said, "Hey, if you think this is a kid's room, you can go fuck yourself. Because an Adult Man lives here now, one who likes *Lizzie McGuire* and NSYNC and *American Idol*, like all grown heterosexuals do." I clicked on a section called "College," obviously, because that's the category all mature men shop for their bedroom posters in. I scrolled through endless images of Pink Floyd covers and Bob Marley heads and that one dumb picture of John Belushi from *Animal House* where he's just standing there with a stupid look on his face, until finally I noticed a subcategory called "Hot Girls" looming in the corner of the screen and, just beneath it, like the shiny clasp of a treasure chest poking through the surface of a dirty beach, waiting for some lucky explorer to catch its seductive glance, "Hot Guys."

I hovered over that link for a good five minutes. I knew full well that the one above it was what other boys, like my older brother, who already had a poster of a woman in some gaudy animal-print bikini hanging on his own wall, would eagerly click without hesitation. But that wasn't what gave me pause. What gave me pause was the gurgling well of Catholic guilt that had been filling my stomach since baptism.

My family was never particularly religious, but by some circumstance we were Catholic, and so, by default, I was sent to Sunday school, where I was taught that anything even vaguely sexual is a sin, and if you even think about sex once in your life, you'll spend eternity personally shining Satan's shoes in hell. Or something like that. I don't really remember specifics, but there are a lot of rules in Catholicism, and most of them go something like this: "No smiling, no getting naked,

no touching your penis for more than five seconds while uri-
nating, no erections, no looking at another person's bare skin,
no kissing anybody but your mother and also Jesus, no meat on
Fridays during Lent, and no looking at posters on the Internet with sinful descriptions like 'Hot.'" And I was a gullible
child, fearful of any semblance of retribution. My cousin once
convinced me that Catholic priests could identify when you'd
sinned and would smash a raw egg on your head when you
approached them during Mass, in front of the entire congre-
gation and everything. And I fucking believed that shit for
almost an entire week before I realized Catholic priests weren't
allowed to touch eggs because they come from bird vaginas.
But still. I was scared shitless.

The truth is, though, I don't remember any chastising
of homosexuality specifically. In Catholic school, all sex is
wrong, no matter who it's with. (Unless you're a priest, but you
know what, I'm not gonna get into that right now.) When I
lingered over that "Hot Guys" link, I wasn't even thinking all
that much about the fact that it was guys, but about the fact
that this was an Adult Thing to do, and something Jesus would
probably not like very much.

Of course, you know where this is going. I clicked the
fucking link. I was thirteen and horny. Catholic guilt might be
able to convince you you're going to hell, but it can't convince
you that looking at dick on the Internet isn't worth the journey.

When I finally opened that page, after asking Jesus if he
would politely look away, it was like Scrooge McDuck saun-
tering into his vault of money, untying his velvet robe, and
skipping the ladder to dive headfirst into his pond of gold. I
should note, for the curious, that these were not high-quality

posters of hot guys (I remain convinced that no such thing exists, though I'd gladly be proven wrong). These were images of burly, misshapen New York firefighters and the midsections of middle-aged bodybuilders and maybe one half-decent picture of David Beckham. Stuff that most grown women, let alone thirteen-year-old boys, would find utterly uninteresting and perhaps even repugnant. And yet, my tiny, horny, sinful brain flooded with adrenaline and dopamine and all those good feelings that say, "If you're looking at a picture of a Latino Chippendale and feeling these things, congratulations, you're a homosexual."

Once the door was open, it was like every little thing reaffirmed the inevitable truth. The shirtless gardener on *Desperate Housewives*, the hot male cheerleader from *Bring It On*, shopping bags from Abercrombie & Fitch, that picture of Mark Wahlberg in his Calvin Kleins, Ashton Kutcher. The first time I heard a song from *Dreamgirls* and the first time I voted for Clay Aiken on *American Idol*. Brendan Fraser in *George of the Jungle* and the Batman movie where Robin wears the pointy-nippled suit. Oh, and the time *Playgirl* published those nude photos of Brad Pitt, which actually happened and wasn't just a concoction of my overstimulated gay brain.

Now, most people mistakenly believe children can't possibly know they're gay, that it's absurd for a child to know that a pubescent fancy for Matthew McConaughey in *How to Lose a Guy in Ten Days* will manifest itself in a lifelong pursuit of a strapping Adonis with well-kept facial hair and a loft-style apartment. And I'd be inclined to agree if the signs on my part hadn't always been so glaringly obvious. I mean, sure, if you don't know you're looking for them, maybe the signals are easy to miss, but it's a goddamn mystery I made it as long as I did without a single member of my family raising questions.

The evidence: I took a baking class instead of playing baseball because I preferred the safe, delicate art of muffin making to the heterosexual demands of running in sand. I stayed inside on weekends to watch TLC's *Trading Spaces* and went to the local library after school to borrow multiple volumes of interior design books to scheme my dream Parisian château. The most emotion I felt on the day of my First Communion was the moment I got a Beanie Baby wrapped in a Backstreet Boys gift bag. I once demanded to be taken to the music store for the sole purpose of purchasing Britney Spears's seminal classic "Oops! . . . I Did It Again" on compact disc. My favorite toys were a collection of animal dolls called "Littlest Pet Shop," which I accessorized to death and kept in a full-sized dollhouse. And my favorite Power Ranger was the pink one, which, I know, isn't gay in and of itself, but considered in context was pretty damn gay.

And yet, my family still claims they had no idea.

The problem, I imagine, is that most of my eccentricities could be ascribed to the fact that I was a shy, chubby nerd who didn't like to talk about his feelings. Sure, I never liked sports or girls or NASCAR (I don't know what straight boys are into), but nobody expects the president of the science club to have a girlfriend. (Actually, to be fair, I did have a girlfriend named Samantha in third grade. And yes, we kissed behind the old car at the end of the block—closed-lipped, on the cheek, I showered in scalding water afterward—and despite the fact that I only truly liked her for the purple, fur-rimmed coat she wore on the playground, to the outside eye, I get that

I was sending hetero cues on this one. But, c'mon, the *Trading Spaces* thing is kinda hard to overlook.) My family, I assume, concluded that I was a hapless, sensitive straight soul who would marry some poor girl when I finally got the courage to talk to her sometime after my fortieth birthday.

And perhaps because I *was* a shy, chubby nerd who didn't like to talk about his feelings, I stayed in the closet through high school and well into college. I suppose a part of me was scared of what the reaction would be, but my family was never particularly conservative. We watched *Will & Grace* and *Glee* and all those shows on HGTV where most of the designers look like they just got off a boat from Fire Island. Our boy dog sometimes humped other boy dogs and my family didn't have him immediately put down.

In retrospect, the real reason I stayed in the closet for so long is that coming out is weird and personal and awkward and, yes, sex-adjacent, and having that conversation with anybody, least of all my parents, was the last thing I wanted to do when I was already weird and awkward and easily embarrassed talking to people about anything vaguely intimate. The thought of having to one day admit, out loud, that I thought I'd maybe perhaps be interested in putting my penis inside another boy's penis (note: this is not how gay sex works or what you're required to say when coming out) was downright terrifying.

Besides, as a teenage boy already self-conscious about my weight and my dorkiness and my all-around social outcastness, I was afraid that coming out would usher in an era of unwelcome attention at a time when I wanted nothing more than to blend in. The only other out gay kid at our high school was a lesbian who called herself Madonna, and she was everything that terrified my teenage self: loud and obnoxious and different and annoyingly confident. If I came out, I feared, I would become Madonna, and gayness would define me.

So I just didn't. And it was easy. I could look at gay posters on the Internet and harbor real-life gay crushes and not have to worry about engaging in embarrassing conversations or attracting any unwanted notice. We lived in the suburbs, after all, which wasn't exactly crawling with other like-minded teenage boys to consummate my gayness with. In fact, the only other boy I was even vaguely interested in was the only other boy I regularly interacted with, one of the neighbor boys, likely an early indication of my predilection for soft-skinned midwestern twinks with muscular calves who are good at baseball and swimming. But, he was straight, and besides, I was a horny red-blooded American boy, and I probably would've fallen in love with a pool noodle if it had slight pecs and asked me to hang out with it after school. (God, this is gonna make going home for Christmas awkward, isn't it? Someone from that family is gonna read this book and make eye contact with me out of their kitchen window, and I'm gonna have to be like, "I'm sorry I admitted to being horny for you/your son/your brother. I was merely a child and also he mooned me once as a joke between bros, so it's kinda his fault for turning on that particular light switch, if you know what I mean.") So I went through high school perfectly content with keeping my gayness not necessarily secret, just not publicized.

It wasn't until college, when I met my straight best friend, the first boy I ever truly loved, and utterly destroyed our friendship with my inability to admit that I was perhaps in love with him in a way he couldn't reciprocate, that I finally felt the pressure to come out and put in the work.

But let's start that story from the beginning.

I met Kellan on the third day of our freshman year of college, at a dining hall table of misfits. (Note: Kellan is not his real name, but it *is* the name of a gay porn star I've seen, so we'll call him that to spare him scrutiny and also to further indulge my fantasies.) By the third day of orientation, my given roommate Troy—a wannabe frat boy with an outsized ego and zero game—having already decided I was a social liability, had ditched me for what he deemed a more lucrative social circle and left me to find dinner alone. I went to the dining hall by myself and walked with my tray to find an empty seat, presumably to plot how I'd spend the next four years in solitude. But I saw an open seat at a table full of guys I recognized from our dorm, and asked if I could join. They said yes.

There was Alex, a moppy-haired engineer who, by day three, had already fully embraced the shower-free, anti-deodorant, sweatpants-and-flip-flops lifestyle of the college professional. Then Jared, a Chinese immigrant studying economics, who always wore jeans that ended four inches above his ankles, and who, I assume, is still wearing the same outfit as he manages some billion-dollar hedge fund on Wall Street. And finally, there was Kellan, Alex's roommate, tall and slender and boyish, with smooth skin and bowl-cut hair, and just the right amount of social anxiety to be approachable. He was beautiful in the same way that nerdy girls in nineties movies are beautiful, which is to say, he was one makeover montage away from being sweep-you-off-your-feet hot, if he actually gave a shit about that kind of thing, but obviously he didn't, because he was too awkward to make that happen.

That night, we all became friends, and ate dinner together for most nights after that. We studied together at night and played video games on the weekends and occasionally smuggled cheap vodka from the junior who lived down the hall, to bring to football games, which was just an excuse to eat cheese fries and be underage drunk outdoors.

A few months in, Alex joined a fraternity (where his disheveled nature would find its true home), so we saw less of him, and Jared was often off on his own (he ate, no lie, approximately seven meals a day, and the rest of us couldn't possibly keep up). So Kellan and I grew particularly close.

One night I mentioned I'd be leaving to go home for Thanksgiving and Kellan let out a dramatic "Nooooo!" and when I asked what was wrong, he said, "You can't leave! Then I'll have nobody to hang out with." And I felt warm and fuzzy and good about the fact that I'd found a friend who considered me his person, another boy who would genuinely miss me when I was gone and rejoice when I returned.

Kellan was an only child, the son of wealthy parents, who spent much of his childhood moving from private school to private school around the world. He'd spent the last several years in Texas, where he'd developed the slightest of southern twangs, but he was, in other words, someone who'd been similarly unaccustomed to deep friendships with other guys. We'd become friends largely out of chance, but we liked each other's company, and worked well together.

You can tell where this is going. It had only been, like, two months and I was already wildly overreading the cues. I knew he was straight, don't get me wrong, but he was sensitive and endearing and he actually liked hanging out with me! I'd never had a close guy friend before—not in adulthood, at least—let alone one who I kinda thought had a nice face and teeth and arms and butt, though I would never admit that, even to myself. And he was a similarly intimacy-averse freak, so romantic rivals were largely out of the equation. In fact, we rarely talked about girls at all. I never mentioned that I was gay (though I'm sure it was obvious), and he never talked all that much about girlfriends, though I knew he'd had one in high school. And so, it was easy to fall into a kind of imaginary romance without having to admit that's what was happening.

And so, we did everything together. Every morning, I would get ready and go to his room to collect him for breakfast (sometimes I'd get there early, because he'd be coming back from the shower and I could see him in his towel). On Christmas break, we'd chat online every day, and being the wildly insecure person I was, I'd often wait for him to chat me first, so I knew he really wanted to talk, and then I'd obviously interpret that as a sign that he was somehow falling in love with me, too. The summer after our freshman year, I flew to Houston to stay with him for a week, and we went to the mall and a baseball game and ate tacos, and we hugged at the airport before I flew home. And one night, when we were both too drunk on Four Lokos (before they were banned by the government), we passed out next to one another on his bed and drunkenly cuddled before falling asleep.

It didn't take long into our sophomore year before I started expecting too much. Actually, that's the nice way of putting it.

The truth is, I went crazy. I became obsessive and possessed. I was in love but didn't want to admit that I was in love, not because I didn't want to admit that I was gay, but because I knew he wasn't, and I wanted our relationship to be the most it could be without us having to say it. We were just best friends! The closest of best friends! The closest you can possibly be to being gay for one another without actually being gay because obviously neither of us is gay, we're just best friends! The tiny gay demon on my shoulder whispered in my ear and made me insane.

I should note, the following behavior is embarrassing to admit, but it happened, and in the interest of full disclosure, I'm copping to all of it. These are the actions of a crazy person, and I am relaying them here so nobody makes the same mistakes as me.

Kellan would want time alone to study, and I would insist on studying together. One day, he would grab dinner without me, and I would spend three days passive-aggressively sulking in my room to teach him a lesson about what it was like to truly be without me. On nights when we'd get drunk on bottles of cheap peach champagne, I'd pretend to fall asleep on his bed, and he'd kick me out, and I'd drunkenly unfriend him on Facebook and send him a lengthy e-mail the next day about how he didn't care about his friends. (And, to be fair, he was sometimes a real insensitive asshole.) We'd make up a couple days later and the cycle would start again.

When he did start a fling with a girl in our dorm—a fact he kept to himself, because, ya know, we didn't talk about intimacy, and also because he probably knew I was becoming a crazy person—I pieced the clues together myself (mutual hickeys spotted in the morning, disgustingly easy to notice) and demanded details, because that's what bros do, right? They tell each other things! About girls! And what they like about girls! And why they like girls so much instead of boys! Friends tell each other everything, even things they don't tell the girls they're secretly hooking up with behind my back!

In perhaps my craziest move, at the depths of my obsession, I wrote an actual essay for an actual class I was taking on Shakespeare using actual evidence from Shakespeare's plays to argue that friendships between dudes are stronger than sexual relationships between dudes and ladies. For real. I really did this. I used academia to convince myself, and the world, that two guys can have a totally normal and not-gay bond that completely transcends the connection between any two human beings ever on earth, and that it's not weird, and that it's totally not homosexual, because Shakespeare said so. (Craziness aside though, that's a real goddamn theory, and it's called "romantic friendship," and Shakespeare was all over that shit. Look it up. Put down this book right now and go read *As You Like It* and then you'll get what I'm talking about. They were totally in love with one another and it totally wasn't gay. Even though there's a bunch of theories today that are like "Nuh-uh! Gays didn't exist yet, so they were totally gay, they just didn't know it was called being gay yet!" But you know what? Fuck those theories. I stand by my essay. I got a B+ on that shit.)

At the culmination of my obsession, I did the thing that I am most embarrassed to admit and cringe most to remember, and before I say it, I implore you to find it in your heart to understand that it made perfect sense in my head at the time, and that the human brain does dumb things when it's in love, even if it refuses to admit that love is what it's feeling.

At the time, there was a girl named Amber. Amber liked Kellan. Kellan liked Amber. They hooked up on the regular. It drove me insane. It wasn't exactly a secret, but they were both embarrassed about it (straight people, always ashamed of their hookups) and, preferring it to go unnoticed, denied it vehemently. Of course, being the crazy person I'd become, I insisted on confirmation, and Kellan insisted on denial, and I'd fall into a hole of exasperation and despair. It wasn't that he was hooking up with some girl, I'd tell myself, it was that he was lying to me about it, even though it was quite obviously that he was hooking up with some girl and only a little bit that he was lying about it.

One night, after we'd all been drinking together in Kellan's room, we said good night and went our separate ways. And then . . . here's where it gets embarrassing and fucked up and cringe-worthy to even think about . . . I waited in the stairwell for approximately three and a half minutes, until I was confident Kellan had left his room to brush his teeth—a ritual he kept religiously every night—and, having heard the "clunk" of the bathroom door, I quietly slunk back into his room, shut the door, and *hid inside his closet.*

Now, I know what you're thinking. "What the fuck is wrong with you, you gay stalker fuck?! You're a grown-ass man who literally climbed inside his friend's closet . . . to do what exactly? Watch him sleep? Catch him masturbating? Filet his skin into tiny bits of jerky? Or were you just trying to be the biggest cock-block you could possibly imagine?"

And the answer is . . . I don't know! I mean definitely not

the filet thing, but still, I don't know! I was gay and crazy and infatuated and jealous and lonely and in denial. I wanted him to love me back! I wanted to be the one who snuck back into his room after everybody had gone away, to tell secrets and make out and fall asleep side by side, and sheepishly left in the morning before the rest of the dorm woke up. I suppose I figured he'd walk back in and I'd jump out and he'd scream so loud he'd turn gay, and then we'd laugh and laugh until we collapsed into one another's arms and fell softly into loving slumber.

Of course, that's not at all what happened. These kinds of things never turn out the way you think they will. What happened next went something like this: I was sitting in that closet, questioning everything in my life that had led to that moment, and the person who walked into the room was not in fact Kellan, but Kellan's we're-definitely-not-hooking-up-even-though-we-totally-are-hooking-up-and-lying-about-it-to-everybody-but-especially-Matt hookup Amber, who had come, I assume, to hook up. I froze. A closeted gay lunatic sitting on the ground of a literal closet. She didn't notice me. She made a phone call to her roommate to say she wouldn't be home that night. She hung up. We both sat in anticipation.

When Kellan returned with his toothbrush, he screamed "GODDAMMIT" the second he opened the door, and for a brief, hopeful moment, I imagined he was pissed to see her, and I would emerge, triumphant, with a look on my face that said, "That's right, you piss worm, he chose me! Now, get out, because we have some intense spooning to do." But his ire, it turned out, was directed at the 230-pound mass that was sticking out from his closet. (Did I mention our dorm room closets were the size of small cupboards and covered in sheer curtains?) Amber screamed when she realized I'd been in there, and they threw me out like they throw out drunks from bars in the movies, roughly, with one hand under each armpit. I'd like to think, at the very least, that I made their night together slightly more uncomfortable, but I suspect events continued as planned.

In retrospect, this is what professionals in the therapy community might call "a great big homosexual cry for help." But nothing much changed after that. I was a strange person to begin with, so hiding in a closet, all things considered, didn't register as insane, at least to the untrained eye, just immature and annoying and something Drunk Matt would totally do because he's a weirdo.

But deep down, I suspect, this was one of many moments when I began plotting my eventual escape into open gayness. At this point, I still hadn't said I was gay out loud to anyone except myself, which seems unbelievable, since I was a twenty-year-old man who listened to Lady Gaga, obsessively watched *The Bachelorette*, and purchased a set of martini glasses to make cosmopolitans in his dorm room. But fear is a powerful thing, and it convinces you that nobody could possibly know your glaringly obvious secret, and that you should keep it a secret, because once you say it out loud, everything will be different. On top of the fear of having to have the awkward, intimate coming-out conversation with my family and the fear of my identity being co-opted by some gay stereotype, there was this new, extra fear of losing my best friend and the person I'd hoped would love me back. He came from a conservative Texas family, after all, and I'd already made it intensely awkward between us without voicing my deep dark gay secret. What would he do once he knew that I was into dudes? Would all of my obviously gay advances register as too obviously gay to tolerate further? I suppose there was a part of me that saw Kellan as an opportunity to come out without having to actually come out. To just skip the awkward, personal, intimate part where you have to tell people you're gay, and jump right to the part where you're getting gay married on a beach in Bora Bora, if only he'd love me back. But coming out is never that easy.

The summer before our junior year of college, Kellan got a girlfriend, and I felt like I was being replaced. My obsession deepened to its darkest point, and again, this is embarrassing to admit, but I stooped low and, at one point, surreptitiously borrowed his phone and glanced at his text messages, which seems like a totally normal thing for a best friend to do (right?!), but when you've already crossed about a thousand boundaries, the other person is rightfully pissed.

We didn't speak for a few weeks.

I decided, finally, that if I ever hoped to have the type of relationship I really wanted with Kellan, like the one that he'd been developing with his new girlfriend, I had to do the thing. I had to come out and be gay and find gay people and do gay things and have faith that the consequences that I feared would be overcome by the rewards of my new fabulous life. And that's the thing about coming out. Before you do it, it feels very much like you're preparing for a kind of metamorphosis. That there will be a Before Gay and an After Gay, and that things will be so massively different that you'll hardly recognize the life you had before.

And it turns out, to a certain extent, that that's true.

So I girded myself for impact. I read books with gay characters to see how they came out. I read *It Gets Better* because that felt like a thing young closeted gay people were supposed to read. I read articles I found on Google about the best way to come out to each person in your life. And finally, I did it.

I wanted my mother to be the first to know, because I knew she would be hurt if I told anybody else something so deeply personal before her. I wrote her a letter, because a letter felt like the easiest and also most dramatic way to do this kind of thing, and I wasn't about to let an opportunity for theatrics go to waste. I don't remember exactly what the letter said, but I think it went something like, "Sorry I ruined a perfectly good set of sheets in the eighth grade. It was because of the shirtless picture of Nick Lachey I saw in the *Us Weekly* you left on the kitchen counter." I cried, and I'm not sure why, because I wasn't sad, but I guess you just cry during these things because it's emotional. Of course, my mother said she loved me and would always love me and she just wanted me to be happy. And, to top it off, one of the first things she asked me was: "Is Kellan your boyfriend?" And I had to fucking say no.

About a week later, I wrote to Kellan and confessed that I was gay, that that's why I'd been so emotional lately, that I was sorry for being a weirdo and hiding in his closet and going through his phone, that he was my best friend and I just wanted to know he would still be my friend no matter what. And, like a good, normal friend, he told me I'd still be the same "Beyoncé loving, Gaga praising" Matt as before, that nothing would change between us.

Of course, coming out wouldn't change the fact that I was

still secretly obsessed with Kellan, even if I tried desperately to deny it. A few days after I told him, I wrote a Facebook message to our group of friends to announce my news, and the following is an absolutely real excerpt from that message. I cringe to reread this message, not to mention publish it for the world to see, but nothing better illustrates the anxieties of my gay brain than these words. Here is that message, edited only for length:

Hey friends,

So I have newsss.

I've been doing a lot of soul-searching this month (haha, not really, I'm just really bored at work), and I have something important to tell ya'll and I could really use your support.

Here it is:

HEY LOOK A BUNNY! (I'm gay) NO REALLY, DID YOU SEE IT? IT WAS A REALLY BIG BUNNY. LIKE, LOTS OF FUR AND EVERYTHING. COULD HAVE BEEN A BIG SQUIRREL EVEN, NOT REALLY SURE. OH WELL, IT'S GONE. YOU MISSED IT.

Phew, now that the squirrel-bunny's gone . . . Yeah, I like dudes. I've always known it—you kinda just know these things. I've known long before I met all of you. But I never told anybody—not my family or friends or anybody—because I was afraid of what everybody would think. I guess I was most afraid that it would suddenly be the only thing people would see about me. I was afraid I would suddenly become the gay kid in the group. And, even if you all had absolutely no problem with me, you would still joke about dicks and assholes and rainbows all the time and I would never hear the end of it. So please don't do that.

And for the record, in case anybody wants to know, I don't have a thing for Kellan, haha, and I never have! Even though I always poke and grab his tiny white butt, I don't want to hit that. (It's a nice butt, don't worry, Kell, nothing to be ashamed of, just not my thing.) It's truly always been meaningless joking. He's my bestie and nothing more. I don't care if I hug him or sleepover in his room or give him a big wet kiss on the cheek. I still don't want his dick. So don't give us shit, got it?

Anyway, that's what I've been up to. Now, if anybody is interested, once we're all together, we can throw a fabulous coming out party, full of foofoo drinks and Beyoncé. Presents are always welcome. And so help me God, if anybody gets me anything phallus shaped, I will not be happy. (Well, maybe a little happy).

Lovelovelove,
Matty B

Phew, there's a lot to unpack here. First of all, the most surprising thing in this entire message is that I was so anxious about being seen as gay that I went so far as to deny myself the pleasure of getting phallus-shaped gifts. See, the thing about coming out is that there is an After Gay, things *do* change, but you start to love it. You start to realize that those pleasures you'd been denying yourself were what would've made you happy all along. Now, several years after this entire mess, the only gifts I will accept are dildos, and I'm profoundly offended if anybody dares to associate me with anything but dicks, assholes, and rainbows. They are deeply entwined in my identity, and I cannot imagine life without them.

But of course, that's hardly the focus of this message. As is painfully obvious to me now, and was painfully obvious to all who read this letter, the only appropriate response to this disaster of a message is "OK, so you're absolutely madly in love with Kellan and clearly want him to fuck babies into you." O. J. Simpson could have written a more convincing denial than this. Birds could have picked up the hints I was dropping. I mean, c'mon! I barely made it two hundred words before bringing his ass into it! It doesn't get any gayer than that.

And so, I replaced one thinly veiled secret for another, and After Gay life began in much the same denial that Before Gay life had ended.

It didn't take long into our senior year for my obsession to reach its inevitable climax. One night, we went out drinking. We came back. I pretended to pass out in his bedroom. He yelled at me to leave. I turned it into a whole thing about how he clearly didn't want to be my friend anymore because he had a girlfriend and because I was gay, and if that's how he was gonna act, then maybe we should just break up. And I dramatically unfriended him on Facebook for one last time and sent him an e-mail the next day saying it was probably best that we just didn't see each other again.

It was silly and dumb, I know, but when you finally release the gay feelings you've been bottling up for twenty years, a few other emotions are bound to come pouring out with the rest. It's a lot like using a plunger to get a hairbrush from the toilet hole. Sure, you'll get your hairbrush back, but that thing's gonna bring some shit back with it. And I wouldn't exactly use it to brush your hair.

Kellan was my first true love, and I regret that the gay demon inside me ruined it all. I'm thankful, in many ways, that I learned enough about myself to know I needed to come out sooner rather than later, that being openly gay was not only an inevitability, but a wonderful thing, that I would not only come out of the closet, but come out of my shell and find my true voice.

Of course, I'd like to think that I simply had no choice but to martyr our friendship to make this discovery, but I know that's not true. The sad lesson here, children, if you haven't yet written me off as a complete sociopath, is that falling in love with your straight best friend is perhaps the worst, most self-destructive idea you could possibly have, because not only will they never love you back in the same way you love them, they'll serve as a constant reminder that you are putting off the thing you should've done years ago but cannot escape. And the only thing worse than your straight best friend not loving you back is spending three years chasing after his affection when you know full well it will never happen.

I spent the rest of my senior year of college going to gay bars in Boystown and drinking pitchers of hard pink lemonade out of straws bent to look like giant dicks. I talked to boys and traded numbers and did all the things that grown gay people are supposed to do. (Buy meth.) After college, I moved to New York, the gayest city in the world, and the first place I'd go where nobody knew any version of me besides the one that was perfectly, openly gay.

I have yet to terrorize a boy quite like I terrorized Kellan (and, if he happens to be reading this, I should say, I'm sorry for, ya know . . . basically everything). But the sappy part of me would like to believe that crazy, closeted Matt is gone, and in his place is someone far happier.

And far less likely to hide in your closet.

ON RELATIONSHIPS, OR TRAITS FOR MY IDEAL MAN

I'm most definitely not an expert on relationships. In fact, I'm like, the opposite of an expert, as all evidence presented in these pages should prove. People have actually begged me *not* to comment on relationships for fear that I'm capable of causing more harm than good. And it's true. The only real relationship I've had in the five years I've spent in New York City was the one I had with the man who delivered my Indian food. He came to my apartment almost every other day, gave me my food, and walked away, leaving only an aura of mystery, sensuality, and a chicken tikka masala dinner special with basmati rice and vegetable samosas. But here's where it got really special, and where I gained the confidence I needed to really dominate this whole relationship thing: about a year into our takeout-fueled flirtations, Indian Delivery Guy started slipping a little extra something into my bag. And that little extra something was a free rice pudding. Now, if I was actually good at relationships, I would've vocalized my feelings better by kindly explaining that I'm more of an ice cream person and think rice pudding has the consistency of cold phlegm. But I appreciated the gesture. And it broke my heart when I moved away from that apartment, never to see Indian Delivery Guy again. For all he knows, I died, choking on a clump of his free rice pudding.

Alas, having been through the intensity of a New York relationship, I know now what I require from a lover and life partner, and have decided to list those requirements on the off chance that someone reading this book may fit the requirements or know someone who does.

TRAITS FOR LANDING MY HAND IN MARRIAGE OR AT LEAST GETTING ME TO EAT IN FRONT OF YOU

1. Can sing with the emotional spirit of a wounded dove and is willing to sing me to sleep every night.
2. Has skin that is soft like the hair of a freshly washed puppy or the underside of a very old toad.
3. Can build a tree house using only his bare hands, three screws, a shovel, and the hopes and dreams of a nation.
4. Can bake an entire three-tier cake, frost it, write an uplifting message on it, and then eat it, all in under an hour.
5. Has the ability when I'm angry to soothe me with only a series of whispers and clicks, like he's calming a spooked horse.
6. Is willing to sing with me at karaoke, but must pretend to be a worse singer than I am, even if he *can*

sing like a wounded dove, and also he must cry when I hit the high notes and pretend like I nail them every single time.

7. Knows how to make pasta with his bare hands and also is maybe good enough to open his own restaurant and name it after me and have a picture of me hanging in the kitchen so when he's old and I'm dead from a carbohydrate overdose, he can stare into my face and remember the times we spent laughing together with mouthfuls of his homemade tagliatelle.

8. Rides a bike to work but isn't all fancy about it.

9. Is willing to read me bedtime stories upon request.

10. Has a psychic ability to tell when I need coffee and is able to supply it instantly when necessary.

11. Sweats only to the point where it's sexy and not to the point where it's all gross and gummy and starts to pool.

12. Knows how to accurately age any wheel of cheese with only a single sniff.

13. Is capable of physically bearing our children in his lush womb.

14. Has hair that isn't too long but long enough to flow in the wind like the strands on a majestic wildebeest running in the African plains.

15. Can play the guitar but never does because one mere stroke of his strings has been said to bring the chilliest of men to irrepressible tears.

16. Capable of wearing a T-shirt and no bottoms without looking like a rampaging pedophile, which is a nearly impossible look to pull off. I mean, have you ever

seen a man with just a shirt on? It's horrifying almost always.

17. Can prepare an entire Thanksgiving dinner alone and feed it to me using only one giant spoon.

18. Can talk to birds, but only to shut them up when they start doing all their bird shit too early in the morning.

19. Can live with someone who will inevitably develop irritable bowel syndrome, if he hasn't already, and have an unhesitating willingness to clean the bathroom on his own whenever necessary, which will be more necessary than most humans would consider normal.

20. Brings me donuts when he goes running in the morning because I'm sure as fuck not gonna get up and go running in the morning, and not just any donuts, but the warm kind from the good place that we went to that one time but whose name I can't remember.

21. Lets me dictate who is big spoon and little spoon every single time with no protests.

22. Brings me free rice pudding.

ON THE STICKY
PERILS OF HAVING
A ROOMMATE

When I was maybe three or four years old, my mother thought it would be a good idea to move my bed into my brother's room and combine our bedrooms into one. That's the thing about having children; you can do these little experiments on them, moving bedrooms and shaking up the social order, and the only consequence is lifelong psychological damage. The reason, at least on its face, was to have a separate room just for toys and games and activities, but I think secretly, her aim was to facilitate bonding between my brother and me. Brothers who sleep in the same room must, she naively thought, grow an unspeakable fellowship.

I was too young to care all that much, but my brother, who is six years older, found the entire arrangement utterly unacceptable (as he should have, if we're being honest), and conspired against it from its very inception. On the first night, just after my mother kissed us good night, turned out the lights, and shut the door, and just as she walked to her own room, admiring her success, my brother sat up in his bed and began whispering a string of terrifying mumblings in my direction. He warned me of clowns that would kill me in my sleep, and werewolves that would devour the remains, and in the morning, there would only be a pile of blood and bones left for Mom and Dad to find in my stead.

I lay there with my eyes as open as they could be, staring at the ceiling, wondering how exactly the clowns would kill me, and if I would feel anything while the werewolves tore my limbs apart, and whether Mom and Dad would scream when they found what was left of me, and finally, I let out a shriek. My brother quickly fell into a sleeping position, and my mother came running back to find my shivering body in a cold sweat for apparently no reason, unable to speak. This went on, uninterrupted, for at least seven whole nights, until finally my mother realized her experiment had failed and relented, pushing my bed back into its room and restoring the rightful balance. But of course, the damage had been done.

Perhaps because of this, I have always placed precious value on my personal space. I rather like having my own bedroom, and spent most of my childhood cultivating a sanctuary. And indeed, I made it all the way to college before ever having to think about sharing my bedroom with another person again. In fact, avoiding having a roommate was a reason I considered not going to college at all. The idea of having to compromise a fundamental part of my worldview for the sake of education was almost too much to handle.

. . .

As most college freshmen are, I was randomly assigned a roommate by an old computer with a terrible sense of irony and humor. Sure, we were told to fill out surveys to gauge our "lifestyle preferences," checking boxes like "I like a clean room," "I like to listen to music while I study," and "I will not stand over my roommate in the middle of the night and whisper lyrics to Whitney Houston's greatest hits." But I'm convinced those surveys were simply a tactic to keep us from rioting when we discovered we'd been matched with someone whose "lifestyle preferences" were practically the polar opposite of our own.

A few months before the school year was set to begin, I got an e-mail announcing I'd been matched with a Troy, and promptly found him on Facebook, which revealed nothing beyond the fact that he was graduating from some preparatory private high school in one of the wealthier Chicago suburbs and was also named Troy.

When I walked in on moving day, Troy had already moved all of his belongings into the room, which appeared to be nothing more than a laptop, two thin pillows, and a duvet, which he was sitting atop, his parents on either side of him, all of them in stern silence. They had the appearance of parents who prized stellar grades and nothing else. Troy sat at attention between them. He was a little shorter than me, but smaller in size, with slight muscles hugging his school T-shirt. He had hair closely cropped to his head, and a sort of blank-looking face, like he was already over it all.

"Hey, I'm Matt," I said. "Nice to meet you." But before I could get any further, my family came bounding in with boxes, bins, and baskets overflowing with clothes, food, and furniture, my mother barking directions about what would go where before she'd even fully entered the room. There were some eight or nine family members who came as part of my entourage, and they worked like an assembly line, carting in the mini-fridge, hanging clothes, making the bed, disinfecting the carpet, and constructing shelving units that would hold all of the shit I'd brought with me, all while Troy's family looked on in stunned wonder. By the time they finished, my half of the room looked like a Bed Bath & Beyond catalog had exploded. Troy's half of the room looked even more depressing in contrast.

We'd only managed to exchange a handful of words, and already I was worried I was making the impression that I was some type of high-maintenance mama's boy—which was technically true, just not something I was eager to advertise twenty minutes into our introduction.

That night, after my circus of a family left and Troy's parents silently slipped away, we went to the dining hall with a handful of our other dorm mates and I started piecing together Troy's persona. He'd wanted to go to another school, he told the group, but got stuck with this one. He wanted to live in another dorm, but they stuck him with this, too. With each new answer, it became increasingly clear that he was trying aggressively hard to seem cool. I was waiting for him to point at me and say, "I asked for a straight albino Jamaican, but they stuck me with you." But that never came.

After dinner, we wandered as a group around campus, hoping perhaps to stumble upon some party. Troy became our group's de facto leader, and we followed him aimlessly, before realizing he had no idea where he was going. Eventually, we all wandered back to the dorm.

That night, after we'd each gotten in bed, he asked me if I was rushing a fraternity. The only thing I knew about fraternities was what I saw in movies: innocent freshmen standing naked in kiddie pools full of Jell-O, humiliating themselves because a bunch of old dudes did the same thing before them, all to live in a grimy old house with fifty other disgusting guys whose rooms smelled consistently like burnt ramen and soggy cereal. Besides, I'd never heard the term "rushing" before, except in the literal sense. I pictured an army of small-muscled freshmen running at an old frat house with lances and spears, like in *Lord of the Rings*.

"No?" I guessed out loud. "I mean, I thought about rushing, obviously. But I don't think it's for me. Are you?"

I could hear him sigh, presumably because he'd gotten his final confirmation that we just weren't going to work out. I don't even think he answered.

. . .

In the days that followed, Troy and I gave up all pretenses that we were anything beyond two random people who happened to share the same two hundred square feet of bedroom. He made his friends, and I made mine. But we'd still occasionally find ourselves at the same dining hall table, and I'd gradually piece together the real Troy. Troy clearly aspired to the stereotypical college boy cliché: party at night, nab some drunk freshman and convince her to give him a depressing hand job in a shower stall, stumble back to the beer-pong table, give a bunch of his dude friends high fives, and eventually pass out in the bushes somewhere behind fraternity row. That was the image he projected at least. But I knew the real Troy, which made his phony frat-boy image all the more insufferable.

For one, he asked me one day a couple months into our year together whether girls could sleep in my bed when I wasn't there. I went home every other weekend (because I was cool), and left behind a perfectly empty bed. So, Troy asked, if I wasn't there, could any of his lady friends use my bed? Of course, the bro thing to do would've been to say "Yes, of course, your strange drunken conquests can totally sleep on my Egyptian cotton, twelve-hundred-thread-count Nate Berkus bedsheets, that's what I bought them for!" But I couldn't get over the image of some blasted freshman throwing up on my memory foam pillows the second Troy pulled down his pants. Besides, I wondered, why would someone as ostensibly accomplished with the opposite sex need a *separate* bed to store his concubines? I wasn't exactly roping in ass myself, but I knew, generally speaking, that sleeping in the same bed was typically part of the deal. So I said no, I'd rather he didn't let anybody sleep in my bed while I was away, or sit on it, or even look at it, because the fabric was too delicate for anybody whose skin composition didn't exactly match mine. He resented me for denying his request, and I resented him for making the request in the first place, ensuring that every time I returned from a weekend away, I'd be forced to sniff my pillows for sweaty residue left by some intoxicated skank.

In any case, I never saw Troy with a girl, which was fine by me, but flew in the face of his air of utter superiority and the clear importance he put on his sexual domination. He'd brag about the women he'd met at this party or that, but as far as I could tell, nothing ever came of it. Of course, I'm not judging the lack of sex. I spent most of my college nights eating shitty pizza, playing video games, and crushing on straight boys from inside the closet. Troy just got on my goddamn nerves, like a hangnail I was forced to live with, a nagging discomfort that grew more and more unbearable each day. I started begrudging the way he smacked while he ate, the pungent smell of his deodorant after he came back from the shower, and his never-ending cough, a dull "HEGH" that I'd thought was from a simple cold when we first moved in, but that persisted day after day for the entire year, a constant "HEGH" "HEGH" "HEGH" every fifteen minutes until I couldn't stand it anymore.

. . .

One Friday night in the spring of our freshman year, I'd just turned off all the lights and gotten into bed. It was a little after midnight, and I was alone, and just about to fall asleep when I heard Troy fumbling with his keys at the door. It was taking longer than usual, and when he finally pushed the door open with a final thud, I could tell he was drunk, the smell of vodka filling the room.

"Oh, shit," I heard him whisper to himself when he noticed I was in bed.

I rolled my eyes in the dark as he struggled to take off his shoes, knocking over a stack of books on his desk. I could hear as he wriggled out of his shirt, wrestled off his pants, the sound of his belt buckle jangling in my ear, and finally plopped down on his bed.

Our beds sat parallel to one another, on opposite sides of the room against facing walls, some eight feet apart, side to side. My back was turned to him, but I could see the wall in front of me light up as he opened his laptop in the dark, the glow of the screen casting a pale glare across the room. I tried to ignore the clacking of the typing, the whirr of the computer fan, the "HEGH" of his coughs. He'd been on his computer before while I was sleeping, his back against the wall opposite me.

But this time the typing suddenly stopped. And then I heard it. The faint sounds of moaning emanating from head-phones, the unmistakable whimpers of some poor actress whose dreams had been so different once long ago, who was left with no choice but to groan her way through a video that ended up in the bowels of the Internet and eventually on the laptop of some college boy who drunkenly stumbled home after strik-ing out for the hundredth night in a row but was nevertheless determined to release whatever pressure he'd spent the evening bringing upon himself. Her muted screams punctuated the room like a tiny subway train screeching along its tracks. "Oh no," I thought to myself, my eyes wide open, staring into the white of the wall in front of me. "This isn't happening." And then, there it was, the distinct sound of palm stroking lotioned flesh, the sound of a wooden spoon mixing a bowl of creamy macaroni and cheese, radiating from Troy's lap.

I lay there in dazed silence, unsure how to process what was happening behind me, or why it was happening, or how to get it to stop.

Now, I certainly don't profess to be an expert at college masturbation, or its protocols, and I certainly don't profess to understand the first thing about straight men, or their curious behaviors, or what exactly they feel comfortable doing in the presence of other men. But I do feel confident enough in my own extensive experience on the subject to point out that there does exist a set of unspoken norms to which all college men implicitly agree, and at the risk of betraying its unwritten nature, they are as follows: always knock before entering a room, or at the very least flounder with your keys at the door for a few seconds to signal that you're about to enter; if possible, post your schedule in public view so your dorm-fellow might better understand which times you'll be away and when you might return; avoid shower masturbation, as it puts strain on dorm plumbing; and by all means—and this one should really, truly go without saying—keep your dick in your pants when another person is in the room, be they unconscious or otherwise!

Perhaps it was my mistake for not laying out these rules more explicitly, I wondered as I lay there motionless, plotting my next move. Maybe I should've gotten Troy to sign some sort of self-pleasure contract, or at least offhandedly mentioned once or twice that I'd appreciate it if he wouldn't lotion up his lap snake while I was lying a couple arm lengths away.

But, there we were, the moans of his chosen film's protagonist struggling to overcome the "squish, squish, squish" of her viewer's strokes. He was making no apparent attempt to hide the fact that this was happening, either so enraptured by his task or so convinced that I was dead asleep across from him. His confidence made me wonder if this had happened before, if perhaps I'd been snoring through night after night of this and had no idea. And sure, while this entire incident sounds like the beginning of every gay porn ever filmed, I still wanted it to end. Nobody wants a masturbating dick they didn't ask for, especially not one that's attached to a vodka-soaked wannabe heartbreaker with a chronic cough.

I'm not one for confrontation, or for awkward encounters, or really for any interactions of any kind. I certainly wasn't about to let him finish, but I couldn't imagine sitting up, looking at him dead in his stupid, slack-jawed face, and telling him to unhand his sausage. So I did the easiest thing at my disposal: I let out a loud, prominent cough, accompanied by some light stirring and grumbling, not quite an "AHEM," but a discernible enough action to send the message: "I am awake. I hear everything. Please sheathe your penis."

Momentarily, the squishing stopped, and I heard the tapping of his finger on the volume key as he lowered the sound of the moaning video. There was silence, and I stirred again, just to say, "Yep. I am totally awake. Let's just everybody put their penises away, and we can get on with pretending this never happened."

The silence lasted, and I let out a sigh that we'd solved the problem swiftly and amicably, with no seed being needlessly spilt.

But the silence lasted only twenty seconds. There came again the "tap, tap, tap" of the volume returned to its previous level, the moans resumed breathlessly from his headphones, and the accompanying "squish, squish, squish" carried on with renewed vigor.

"OH MY GOD," I screamed in my head. "NOW WHAT?"

Still determined to solve this without having to actually acknowledge that I'd been awake this whole time, I took drastic action. I started to roll over. Until then, I'd been steadfastly facing the wall, giving Troy all the privacy of my turned back. But surely if I turned to face him, even with my eyes still closed, he'd have to stop. No man in his right mind would take that kind of risk.

And so I rolled, more dramatically than I normally would, grumbling and fumbling like an old man looking for the glasses atop his head, coughing for extra measure to indicate full alertness. When I finally landed on my other side, facing Troy's direction, I noticed he'd stopped yet again. Frozen, I imagined, like a deer in the glow of his laptop.

For five whole minutes, there was nothing but the sound of the whirring computer fan and the occasional click of his touchpad. Glorious silence. I started to focus on falling asleep, wondering how I'd recount this story at breakfast tomorrow.

But sure enough, the subtle moans rang out again, and the "squish, squish, squish" continued, now more strenuously than before, like he was rushing to get it over with, angry at having been interrupted.

Finally, I rolled onto my back and stretched out my arms above me, letting out an obnoxious yawn, like I was stirring myself from a particularly good dream but wasn't quite awake. This had to end, but I still refused to acknowledge that I was fully awake, intent as I was on avoiding the awkwardness as much as possible. And so I leaned forward, pretending to be half-asleep, and reached into the mini-fridge for a bottle of water, which I opened and chugged unpleasantly. If convincing him I was awake wasn't enough, I figured, maybe my slobbering would kill his libido entirely.

Meanwhile, Troy had shifted his pillows to obstruct his exposed lap, and the squishing had abated. I maintained the pretense of being half-asleep, fully vertical in bed with the bottle of water still dripping on my lap, but my eyes still closed. I made an exaggerated effort to reach for my cell phone and lay back down, facing the wall, with my phone illuminated against my face. There would be no mistaking now that I was awake.

Defeated, I heard Troy shift on his sheets, pulling his boxers back up, and then the sound of him stumbling toward the door and down to the bathroom, presumably to complete whatever business he had to attend to.

Vindicated, I turned off my phone. And in beautiful silence, I was able to finally fall asleep.

In the days that followed, Troy gave off very little indication that he knew what had happened, or at least managed to convince himself he'd been stealthier than he had been. Though, of course, I wouldn't expect him to walk in and say, "Hey, that was crazy last night, wasn't it?!" But it would've been nice to detect at least a hint of shame in place of his typical bravado.

I didn't hesitate repeating the story to my friends the next morning: the Almighty Ladies' Man, Troy, staggering home on a Friday night, drunk and dejected, vigorously massaging his neglected manhood. I happily admitted to being the unwitting dope in this story, if only to expose Troy and his shameless semi-public masturbating.

. . .

One afternoon, not long after The Night of the Incident, Troy stopped me in our room. A rare moment of communication.

"My parents are coming this weekend," he said. "They want to take us out to brunch."

It wasn't a question, more a delivery of an uncomfortable fact that neither of us wanted to hear, like announcing that a nearby nuclear plant just exploded.

"Oh," I said back, and then, without thinking, "Um. Sure. I'll be around."

Goddammit. Why, in this moment, I didn't think to come up with an excuse—literally any excuse—is beyond me. This is what I do. I panic. I say yes to things. I can't say no, especially not to food. What was I supposed to do now? I considered driving my bike into traffic just for a believable pardon.

"Oh, OK. Cool," Troy said. I could tell he was thinking the same thing. I wasn't supposed to say yes. He was just delivering the message, one I'm sure his parents forced him to deliver. Either that, or all of his other friends were too obnoxiously fratty to bring around, and I was simply the safest option. As far as they knew, I was Troy's only friend.

When the weekend came, we walked silently to the only brunch place in town, where his parents were waiting. They were just as serious-looking as the first time I'd met them, on move-in day nearly a year ago. Stern and intellectual. Both doctors.

The entire meal, Troy barely spoke more than a few sentences, lifting his eyes from his plate only to stick his knife in the cup of butter or to take a sip of orange juice. It felt like we'd all just gone to the same funeral.

"So, I'm gonna have to be the one who turns this meal

around," I thought. "Just like I fix everything in this relationship."

For the rest of the meal, I spoke to Troy's parents as if they were my own, regaling them with stories of our inseparable friendship, the nights we spent keeping one another awake, watching movies, and comforting ourselves to sleep.

What can I say? I know how to work for a free meal.

. . .

A month later, as the school year was coming to an end, and my time with Troy was finally almost over, I had my own moment of drunken weakness.

By then, I'd been selected as the dorm historian, a meaningless role that had only one responsibility: writing the dorm newsletter. Except the newsletter wasn't actually a newsletter, but an *Onion*-like page of satire taped to the back of the dorm's bathroom stalls. A dumb piece of potty-time entertainment that fell to me.

For the last issue, I drank perhaps a few too many sips of cheap boxed wine while I was writing, and concocted a list, cleverly titled, "Things Not to Do While Your Roommate Is Sleeping." In my defense, for the most part, the list was entirely innocent. At least 90 percent of it had absolutely nothing to do with Troy. Things like "Don't eat a bag full of cured salamis and cheeses" and "Don't perform maintenance on your personal pubic hedges, no matter how aggressively your freakishly pubescent body parts have begun to shed their fur." And of course, being the drunk asshole that I can be, I added as a final touch, and in caps for unmistakable emphasis: "And most important, DON'T MASTURBATE WHILE YOU THINK YOUR ROOMMATE IS SLEEPING. TROY, I'M TALKING TO YOU. I KNOW WHAT YOU DID."

Save. Print forty copies. Tape to the back of forty bathroom stalls. Wait to be murdered.

Now, before you write me off as a terrible asshole who broke some kind of deep, unspoken code about never tattling on your midnight-masturbating roommate, it was ostensibly a newsletter full of satire! At the very worst, everybody should've assumed I was making a horrible joke, except for all of the people I'd told the truth, which included basically everybody.

Regardless, Troy never mentioned it, either because he never shit in our dorm, or because he pretended, as always, he was too cool to care.

In any case, Troy was the last man I ever (reluctantly) shared a bedroom with. And I hope this story stands as a warning to any man who may consider sharing a bedroom with me in the future: Let it be known that this is my territory. What happens here is in my control.

And if you try to secretly masturbate behind my back, I *will* tell everybody we know that it happened.

ON LIVING ALONE
IN NEW YORK CITY

There's a point in the process of searching for an apartment in New York City, perhaps when you're standing in a paper-bag-turned-bedroom, staring at a toilet beneath a kitchen sink next to an icebox plugged into a power strip that's dangling from a hole in the wall, when you start to wonder if death might truly be the answer. A coffin costs less for the same square footage, after all. It's got hardwood finishing, with bedding and draperies already installed, no year-end rent increases, no neighbors to complain that the TV is too loud, a solid foundation, and most important, no roommates to judge you for decaying in the same spot all weekend. It's really the perfect arrangement, all things considered.

But a coffin isn't always the answer, which is how I found myself, like millions of would-be New Yorkers every year, in search of a place my living, breathing body could occupy for less than the cost of sacrificing my firstborn. (Though, to be fair, I'd gladly sell my unborn children to a labor camp in exchange for a two-bedroom Greenwich Village loft with a washer and dryer.)

I first moved to New York City four years ago, and by most standards, my first apartment—in the deep Brooklyn neighborhood where Meryl Streep's character lived in that movie where she kills one of her kids—was an absolute mansion. I had a bedroom that fit both a mattress and pillows, a bathroom with a mirror, and a kitchen with a window. The neighbors I shared a wall with only had vigorous animal sex once in three years, as far as I could hear. And I found only one or two cockroaches, near the refrigerator, but they were both already dead, so that basically doesn't even count. Any apartment in New York with a mirror, a window, and a mysterious air for killing cockroaches is luxury living.

Of course, like many New Yorkers, I had a roommate: a former college classmate named Lindsey who is too pure for this world, and certainly too pure for the havoc I wrought upon our bathroom and kitchen. For three shared years, Lindsey generously cleaned our common spaces every week with no help from me. Which I justified by reasoning that she actually must really enjoy cleaning—and she did, I could see it in her eyes—but the truth is, I was lazy and she wasn't, and every time I said I would get around to cleaning the toilet, she would rightfully call my bluff and clean the damn thing herself. Besides, I barely left my bedroom or made our apartment feel like anything more than a hole that I hibernated in when I wasn't out getting drunk.

I was an awful roommate and an even worse person, but

Lindsey never called me out on it. She just channeled her disapproval into cleaning the toilet and letting the shiny spotless porcelain bowl speak for itself. The guilt I felt for imposing my monstrous lifestyle on someone as genuine and gentle as her was too much to bear. I ended our three years of shared mansion living and began my search for a private nest I could destroy guiltlessly on my own.

There are a lot of factors to consider when trying to find a new apartment, especially if you, like me, spend twenty-three hours a day decomposing indoors. Your apartment walls have to contain your sounds and smells, your door must be thick enough to ensure any potential callers always assume you're not at home, and your neighbors must be of the kind that are prepared to see a specimen like yourself emerge Gollum-like once daily to retrieve carbohydrates and alcohol.

Finding an apartment means you have to find the answers to a laundry list of questions that at first seem entirely unimportant, but prove to be the most important questions of all. Like: How cute are the local Starbucks baristas? Can you imagine yourself carrying out a sordid love affair with the tallest, handsomest one, communicated only through messages drawn in cappuccino foam atop your daily lattes? Will he find you the day you decide to move away and tell you that he wants you to stay—no, he *needs* you to stay—because he can't imagine his life without you, can't imagine what his days would be like without your smile walking through those doors every morning?

These are the types of questions they don't tell you to ask. *But they matter.*

Also: How shirtless is the local running community? How often does the Italian family who lives next door use an entire head of garlic to make marinara sauce for breakfast? Do the tenants who live directly above your prospective unit own an elephant or other large elephant-like animal with diabetes, causing it to roam across the hardwood floors multiple times a night to relieve its diseased elephant-sized bladder? And perhaps most important, what size towel do the neighborhood bachelors use to wrap themselves post-shower, and how thin are their bedroom curtains?

Armed with the right questions, I tried at first to find an apartment on my own. If I was gonna strike out on my own, I figured, I should really go for it. Brokers, after all, are a sleazy breed of human who don't give a shit whether you live or die. They'll gladly sell your dream apartment to the couple waiting behind you with their IKEA bed frame at the ready, prepared to swoop in and claim the room you planned to masturbate in for their own perverted pursuits, like having sex with each other at the same time. Like monsters.

But you realize how quickly and drastically you're willing to drop your standards when you try anything on your own. Poring through Craigslist, I found only one listing in my price range, albeit one I found virtually impossible to refuse. It was a luxury downtown loft, furnished to perfection, and completely free. The only catch: in exchange for free room and board, the man listing the apartment demanded to spoon-feed his tenant three meals per day.

"Look," I told my parents, "it's got exposed brick walls, stainless steel appliances, a Whirlpool bathroom, and it's all *for free*. And it comes with three meals every single day, and I won't even have to feed myself. I'll never have to worry about going hungry again."

But that day, some guy got killed by some other guy because they met on Craigslist, or something equally violent and tragic, and of course, that was the one night my parents decided to watch the news. And then suddenly everyone on Craigslist offering a free apartment in exchange for spoon-feeding their tenant three meals a day must be a killer.

I tried telling them everyone in New York City is a potential murderer. I mean, that's sort of this city's deal. Lindsey probably tried killing me in my sleep plenty of times, and I survived living with her for three whole years. What's a guy with a spoon fetish gonna do? Feed me to death?

But I was forced to relent. I abandoned both my hopes for a generous apartment sugar daddy and the prospect of successfully finding an apartment alone.

So I hired a broker named Pam recommended by a friend. Pam was an older, oversized woman, in her sixties, who moved like she was running away from a very small, very sluggish axe murderer, which is to say, she barely moved at all, but in a very urgent way. She took deep breaths in the middle of her sentences, and spoke cautiously, like someone was listening to our conversation. Her attention was always half-focused on what was happening around us, and so she never quite seemed to notice what I was saying.

"I thought you were supposed to be a girl" was the first thing she said to me, outside the building where we'd planned to meet.

"Oh. Um. No? I'm a dude," I said. I'd texted her I was "Arielle's friend Matt, and I'm looking for an apartment," but

I realize now I might not have been clear enough. "Is that . . . gonna be a problem?" I asked her then.

She shrugged her shoulders and heaved herself inside anyway. I followed along, uncertain. We climbed into the elevator together.

"You're the first one to see this apartment," she huffed. "The landlord didn't get me the keys until today. A piece of work, he is." She turned to me and made sly eye contact. "The kind of guy who beats his wife, ya know?"

I opened my mouth, but no words came out. I mean, what the fuck are you supposed to say to something like that? The "kind of guy" who beats his wife? *Does he beat his wife or not, Pamela?* If he does, why are you so casual about this? If he doesn't, what the fuck are you talking about? I looked at the ground. "Oh. Uh. OK. That's . . . that's something."

We didn't say anything else. The elevator doors opened, and Pam led me twenty feet down the hallway to the apartment. She burst through the door and collapsed immediately onto the closest piece of furniture she could find, out of breath from the taxing elevator ride and stroll. Granted, we were on the eighth floor, and it's possible the high altitude was harsh on her feeble lungs. "Make yourself useful and turn on the air conditioner," she barked.

I did as she asked, and left her to defrost while I reviewed the apartment, though there wasn't much to review. It was a one-room studio, big enough to fit a small bed, a couch, and a dying old woman without feeling too crowded. There was a tiny bathroom and a kitchenette, and two windows that faced a solid brick wall, so nobody could see in or out.

Pam's phone rang and she answered. She spoke to the other

person for five minutes, hung up, and turned to me. "One of my friends just died." Breath. "He was like a mentor to me." Breath. "Anyway, you want this apartment or not?"

I paused for a second. I looked around for hidden cameras. And then I told Pam no, I wasn't interested in this beautiful litter box of an apartment, but maybe the next one, and also are you sure your blood pressure isn't dangerously low today, because that's the only fucking explanation I can fathom for a woman behaving as strangely as you are, except I didn't say any of that because I'm too polite, I just said, "No, thank you, ma'am. Now please can we go before you murder me?" And then we left.

The next day I got too drunk at a bar, probably because it had been forty-eight whole hours since I'd started looking for an apartment, and I hadn't found one yet, and I was ready to die. I was slumped at a table, my friend Jennifer standing fifteen feet away at the bar.

"Bring me water, homo," I texted her. She didn't immediately reply, so I texted her again. "DON'T BE A HOMO-PHOBE. BRING ME A WATER." Drunk Matt assumes the worst of people very quickly. Still no response, I texted her a third time. "Why do you hate gays?!" Nothing.

A few minutes later, she walked over to the table and sat down. "Why aren't you answering my texts?" I slurred.

"Because you didn't text me," she said.

And that's when I realized I hadn't been calling Jen a raging pro-dehydration homophobe. I was calling Pam the Broker a raging pro-dehydration homophobe. "OH MY GOD!" I screamed. "I THOUGHT I WAS TEXTING YOU!"

"OMG I'M SO SORRY," I texted Pam the Broker. "I DON'T THINK YOU HATE GAYS."

But she never replied. And I never heard from Pam the Broker again.

The next week, I found Pam's replacement, a broker named Mark. He looked suspiciously like Mr. Clean if Mr. Clean had served time in a federal corrections facility for cooking meth. His shiny bald head was punctuated by bulging skull veins and his biceps were kept at a solid 75 percent flex at all times. In truth, I chose him because I was too scared not to choose him. Somehow, I thought, he'd find me and rent me an apartment and make me move there whether I wanted him to or not.

But Mark, like Pam, proved to be a person of many oddities. On our way to view our first apartment, he stopped me midsentence to ogle two women passing us on the sidewalk. "Sorry, buddy," he said. "I just get so distracted by beautiful women. You understand, though." I most certainly did not.

The apartment we found was smaller than the one Pam showed me but livable enough, and Mark's biceps seemed to throb in approval. Sure, it didn't have an oven or a fully closable bathroom door, and the toilet was barely bigger than one of those training potty seats parents use to put on top of normal-sized toilets to teach their babies how to shit like civilized humans. But whatever. I was running out of time, and Mark's skull veins weren't getting any calmer. Two days later, I was signing a lease. (Along with a piece of paper that said I'd promise not to lick the walls. For real. The lease agent said it was totally standard. "Just a little thing that says you won't sue us if you chew on the windowsills," he told me. I signed it, but still. It's a pretty fucked-up thing to ask of someone. I should be free to chew on whatever I want to in my own apartment.)

I finally had my own apartment to destroy at will, which is perhaps the greatest feeling in the world—to have the freedom to debase a space that belongs to you (however temporarily) in the manner you wish to debase it. There's nothing greater than sitting on furniture with your bare ass knowing that it's *your* furniture to defile, or pissing into an unwashed toilet you know is being seasoned like a skillet with every use, or spilling an entire bowl of cereal in bed, knowing you can ball up the sheets, toss them down the trash chute, and buy new ones the next day with not a single soul to judge you for it. Finding an apartment in New York City is perhaps the greatest struggle, but it yields the greatest and simplest reward.

ON
SELF-SUFFICIENCY

I spend a lot of time thinking about how I will almost definitely be the first one to die in the apocalypse. It's kinda hard *not* to think about the end of the world when you live in New York City, considering there's already a very fine line between order and chaos here, and all it really takes to send us into primitive panic is a delayed subway train, an inch of snow, or a giant ball of glitter falling in Times Square on New Year's Eve. Anybody who's shopped at the Target in Brooklyn knows there are very few rules keeping New York society from descending into all-out bloodshed; I tried returning a microwave there once, and left with three arrow wounds, a snakebite, and Dutch elm disease, which is technically a disease for trees, but apparently not at Target, because nothing matters at Target, especially not the one in Brooklyn. Trust me when I tell you, if the apocalypse strikes New York, whether by way of aliens, zombies, or pandemic, it would take Manhattan less than one hour to burn itself to the ground. (Everybody in Brooklyn, I assume, would die in the initial invasion.) Give us one sighting of a convincing UFO, and we'd all kill one another in the toilet paper aisle at CVS long before CNN told us it was only a stray Goodyear blimp.

And yes, I know for a fact, I would be the first one to die.

It's not for lack of preparation. I've thought about which of my neighbors' dogs is likely to be the most nutritious and how many bottles of whiskey I could drag back to my apartment in one liquor haul. I know where my closest nuclear fallout shelter is, and I know exactly which apartments in my neighborhood are the most expensive and most likely to satisfy my dream postapocalyptic life of luxury. But mostly, I think about the fact that I would absolutely not make it long enough for any of that to matter.

There's really no end-of-the-world scenario I can imagine where I'm not the first to go. If aliens invaded, they'd know right away that I'm not strong or coordinated enough to keep as a human slave and that my body is far too ravaged to conduct any meaningful experiments on. I mean, if you're a superior alien race ransacking earth for servants and test subjects, you're not gonna kidnap a three-hundred-pound homosexual with seasonal depression and hay fever. If a zombie virus struck, I know my luscious, doughy body would be too irresistible to go undetected on the streets. (I have no doubt that my layers of fat have created the perfect marbling and that I would be absolutely delicious.) If a contagion swept the country, I know my immune system would put up almost no fight. And I know I'm barely tough enough to defend myself against a robot vacuum, let alone a robot army, should one suddenly rise against humanity. I know that I can't run fast enough to stay out of reach, that I take far too many naps to stay alert for danger, and that my past experience with group projects would make it impossible for me to live in a community of survivors without having a meltdown resulting in my inevitable exile.

But the real problem—the one that would almost certainly get me killed long before the nuclear radiation charred my body from the inside out—is that I have absolutely no conceivable real-world skills. I can't defend myself. I can't cook for myself. I can barely gather supplies. The contents of my fridge is currently four cans (yes, cans) of sparkling wine, an expired carton of milk, and a plastic container of sliced watermelon that I bought because I find cutting my own watermelon to be too much work. In my cabinets, there is only a single box of brown rice that I never finished because brown rice is disgusting and an old bag of stroganoff noodles that I bought for a slow cooker recipe but never bothered to cook because slow cookers make you think about what you want to eat for dinner ten hours in advance, and I can only think about what I'm eating as it's entering my body. The only things I am well stocked in are whiskey and face moisturizer, and I can't exactly eat either of those. If the world came crashing down right this moment, I'd have enough supplies to last a few hours at best before I'd be forced to go out into nature, where I'd be inevitably mauled, eaten, or enslaved.

How did I turn out this way, you ask? I ask myself that question every time I try opening a jar of maraschino cherries or undertake even the most basic of home improvement tasks. I tried installing a curtain rod with a power drill by myself and somehow bored five holes in the drywall before

I got exactly the right spot. And that's a wall! A completely motionless target! You think I *chose* to be this inept? No. It was bred into me.

I come from a long line of unabashed weaklings, incubating for decades in the comfort and safety of midwestern middle-class suburbia. My father, who could have spent his time teaching me to hunt venison and identify nonpoisonous berries, spent the lion's share of his spare energy collecting antique clocks. Hundreds of them. You don't learn real-world skills from a guy who collects antique clocks. I mean, sure, he could barter the hell out of a cuckoo clock at the flea market, but that's not gonna save us from roving bands of postapocalyptic motorcycle-riding cannibals. And my mother, finding everything to be a danger, left us ill-prepared for greater threats. When you grow up thinking a mouse is the most dangerous thing in the world, what happens when you encounter a guy with a baseball bat covered in barbed wire?

Case in point: Chicago, winter 1999, one of the worst winter storms to hit the city in recorded history. In the course of a day, almost three feet of snow fell on Chicago and the surrounding suburbs, and in the days after, temperatures reached lows of minus twenty degrees Fahrenheit, which the National Weather Service categorized as "extremely fucking cold." It was one of those storms where the weatherman goes outside with a bucket of boiling water, throws it at the sky, and watches as it freezes before it hits the ground. It's a fun little way of saying, "We're all going to fucking freeze to death, but at least our bodies will be well preserved."

As is often the case when a storm of this magnitude hits, power and phone lines were downed and we lost electricity.

As was *not* often the case, we lost power for not just a few hours, but *five entire days*. That's five whole days with no heat, no lights, no telephone, no hot water, no microwave, and no access to my AOL account. We lived on a dead-end street, which meant no snowplows could forge a path to set us free, although that didn't matter much because every car on the block was almost entirely encased, and the front and back doors of our house were snowed shut. We were, quite literally, buried alive. The only way we could let out the dog to pee was by opening a window and slowly lowering her to the ground with a leash and harness.

Now, let me reiterate, we were not a strong family. We relied overwhelmingly on machines to do our brawniest tasks. If we'd all been alive a century and a half earlier, and attempted to brave the Oregon Trail, all of us, including our oxen, would've died from dysentery less than a mile from our house, I'm absolutely sure of it. My family could barely survive driving to a restaurant in the same car; we wouldn't have lasted thirty minutes in the same covered wagon. And now we faced our very own winter apocalypse.

For five nights, we struggled to keep from freezing. We melted snow on the gas stovetop to use as bathing water. We ate what meager food we had by candlelight. After dinner, I played with my rag dolls and pig bladder balloon while Papa played songs on his fiddle. At night, we all slept in the same room to conserve heat, an arrangement that included our two hamsters, Muffin and Biscuit, whose cages we covered in blankets to keep them from icing into tiny hamster steaks.

As the fifth night began, I'd started to think our supplies had finally reached their end. My body would be found frozen to the floor, clutching my Beanie Baby collection. Archaeologists would conclude I was trying to keep them warm in a final act of selfless love. Museum exhibits would be built about me. "NAMELESS GINGER CHILD FOUND CLENCHING HEAP OF GAY STUFFED ANIMALS. A DISSECTION OF HIS STOMACH FOUND ONLY STRAWBERRY POP TARTS AND EGGOS."

But, on this very night, just as I was closing my eyes in a peaceful acceptance of frozen death, our neighbors managed to pound away enough ice to knock on our front door and offered to share their spare generator. Apparently they'd been using one since the storm first knocked out the power and had been living in comparative luxury less than twenty yards from where I'd been sizing up which hamster would be the most delicious. (Muffin, because she was a girl and had more voluptuous, meaty hips.)

And so, we were saved. Without the kindness of strangers or the aid of a magic electricity machine, we would surely have died and our corpses preserved like the charred victims of that volcano that killed all those people in ancient times. I mean *probably*. I'm sure we were totally fine, and my parents will read this and be like, "That never happened, we knew exactly what we were doing, why are you always like this?" But I was nine years old, and it felt like we were definitely gonna die, and the fact that I *thought* we were definitely gonna die should be proof enough that I clearly wasn't absorbing any meaningful survival skills. Because that snowstorm was only the beginning of a long series of instances in which my capacity for mastering basic survival skills would be tested.

Later that same year, I took my girlfriend to the park,

and yes, you'd think that a nine-year-old homosexual having a girlfriend would be the direction I'm going with this, but it's actually not, so just get that right out of your head. I was nine years old and she had good clothes and nice hair and agreed to be my girlfriend, so it was absolutely real. Yes, the fact that I didn't know I was gay yet maybe foretold my lack of simple intuition, but that's not really the focus here. We were on a kid date. We rode our bikes to the park together, and held hands on the swings, and it would've been a perfectly magical afternoon had we not been confronted by a drifting gang of fifth-graders determined to ruin our budding heterosexual romance.

I don't know why these fifth-graders were so intent on ruining our park date, besides the fact that children are trapped in a Darwinian struggle for a higher place in the playground hierarchy, which makes them unusually vicious and cruel. These children were no exception.

Their leader, a skinny but muscley eleven-year-old named Kyle who I'm pretty sure does meth now, approached me and shouted something like, "AWWW. ARE YOU ON A DATE WITH YOUR LITTLE GIRLFRIEND?!" And I had to be all like, "Um, technically we're not putting any labels on it right now, we're just kinda testing things out and exploring our likes and dislikes—" But before I could finish, he started lunging at me like a pimply jaguar pouncing on a portly, defenseless antelope, and I had to react.

Now, this is the point where most humans would mount some semblance of a defense, if not for their safety then at least for their dignity. But I was never taught to fight. My idea of self-defense was to simply avoid danger by never leaving the house. My parents never had to worry about teaching me to defend myself because I was rarely ever in nature long enough to put myself at any reasonable risk. (That being said, I guarantee you neither of my parents can throw a punch.)

So I did the only thing I knew how to do well: I froze. I stood frigid with my hands glued to the sides of my hips like I'd been tied up with invisible rope and waited for impact. When his body collided with mine, I fell to the ground like a toppled tree. And I lay there motionless, with his body on top of mine, hoping that if I remained inanimate long enough, he'd think he'd killed me and would move on to his next target.

And surprisingly, it worked. He got up while I stayed on the ground with my eyes closed, waiting for death. He and his friends rode away, and I waited until their distant laughter dissipated before I got up, dusted myself off, grabbed my handbag, and rode home silently beside my heterosexual partner. I'd like to think my bully believed my possum act, but more than likely, he took pity on my lifeless body and realized I was too pathetic of a conquest to punish further. Either way, I survived, but only barely.

I tell this story not for your pity, but to show you how I behave in the midst of confrontation. When presented with the choice between fight or flight, my body is totally like, "You know what? Let's just shut it down. Let's just shut this whole thing right on down and reconsider whether it's even worth it."

Maybe you're like, "It's OK, Matt. Plenty of people can't fight, but surely you could still weasel your way through the apocalypse like a coward!" But this presumes I have other tested real-world skills.

Even if I *did* manage to fight my way to the grocery store

for supplies, I sure as hell wouldn't know what to do with them. I haven't cooked a meal for myself in nearly six months, because last time I tried cooking my apartment smelled like burnt broccoli for twelve agonizing days and I refuse to go through that again. The only successful time I used an oven, I baked a batch of delicious sugar cookies (the Pillsbury kind that you literally just plop on a tray and throw angrily in the oven when you want cookies but you're too lazy to care about life), and when I left them on the kitchen table to cool, an aggressive New York squirrel busted his way through my window and stole them right from the plate. Even when I succeed at basic tasks, my work is easily undone by even the least formidable opponent. I have no doubt, if the apocalypse hit tomorrow, that a squirrel would eat me well before any human had the chance.

And if you think I'd be able to domesticate an animal of my own to help in my defense, well, consider that I've killed almost every pet I've ever been charged with raising. The first pet I had, a beautiful goldfish named Margaret that I'd convinced my parents I was responsible enough to keep alive, lasted less than one week before she died in an apparent suicide. Turns out, I was too proud of Margaret, and lugged her bowl from my bedroom every time guests visited, so I could show her off, but apparently sloshing a goldfish up and down two flights of stairs every day doesn't provide for the most hospitable of aquatic environments. Rather than endure the tempest I created for her daily, Margaret went on a hunger strike and was found belly-up one afternoon when I went to fetch her for her Wednesday walk. Even Muffin the hamster didn't last very long, though she died of what we think was an abdominal tumor that I couldn't possibly have been responsible for. But I still probably had something to do with it.

So no, I do not think I would survive the apocalypse. It's amazing I'm even able to stay alive without the apocalypse. Give me the slightest hurdle to jump over, and I guarantee you it kills me before my feet have the chance to leave the ground.

ON KEEPING
A CLEAN AND
TIDY APARTMENT

1. Dusting is something you only do if you don't yet realize that dust is a lie perpetuated by the feather industry to make us believe rubbing dead goose wings on our furniture will make them clean. Guess what, feather industry? Furniture is like a cat. It basically cleans itself.

2. Likewise, a shower is a self-contained germ vacuum, and only requires an occasional light rinsing or heavy spitting on. I mean, have you ever heard of someone actually *cleaning* their shower when they're in there basically every day with shampoos and conditioners and shaving creams? I don't think so.

3. It's only *really* necessary to clean your bathroom once over the course of a year, because, think about it, the cave people didn't clean their bathrooms at all. They just shit outside. And they could kill, like, whole mastadons. Not cleaning the bathroom made them stronger.

4. A window basically half-belongs to the person on the other side of it, which means you only have to clean windows half as often as you think you should, and the rest of the time is someone else's problem.

5. Sweeping the floors and/or mopping is unnecessary if you wear the right kind of socks.

6. If you can't see the mess, it doesn't exist, which is why baby Jesus invented shag carpeting, closets, and the space between couch cushions.

7. Clothes can be reworn as often as the wearer can stand his own stink, which means laundry is basically always optional as long as you can convince yourself the smell of your own waste is less offensive than the idea of walking to the nearest washing facility.

8. If you leave the garbage sitting in one spot long enough, it'll eventually be able to take itself out.

9. All dishes are like cast-iron skillets: if you don't wash them, each use adds a new layer of delicious seasoning to your next meal.

10. Don't listen to what the "experts" tell you. Sponges last forever.

ON NOT BEING
THE PEOPLE'S
CHOICE

When I was a child, being on TV was the greatest possible thing that could happen to a person.

One summer, while I was at my aunt and uncle's house, a drunk driver drove into a house down the street, directly through the wall and into the living room. We heard the crash from a few blocks away and went running to see what happened. Everybody was safe, except for the living room set, I imagine, but it was a big enough disaster to attract the local news community, and soon enough, vans with satellites started rounding the corners, parking along the curb, and hauling out cameras and tripods. It was a spectacle. This was the suburbs, after all. Nothing exciting happened here to begin with, and now there was something besides a television set or bonfire for all of us to stand and stare at. There were lights, and microphones, and local news reporters furiously dabbing makeup on their sweaty foreheads. All to look at a car that was sitting motionless halfway through a brick wall. But still, whenever one of the camera's lights went bright, my cousins and I would walk aimlessly behind the reporter, far enough away to seem innocuous, but close enough so our faces were clearly captured on screen. Even then, I knew how to find my light.

That night, we taped every eleven o'clock news program—who the hell knows which station's cameras we were standing in front of—and the next morning, we went through every tape until they got to the segment about the car, and while the reporter droned on about the damage and how the car would be removed and what hospital the driver was spending the night in, we looked for a hint of ourselves in the back corner, a wisp of hair or even a shadow. In the end, none of us made it on air. Television cameramen are well equipped to crop out menacing children like us. But still, the prospect of getting our fifteen minutes of fame was tantalizing. We could've been stars!

I never quite understood this desire to be on television, at least in this way. This was before the Internet was anything beyond instant messaging and chat rooms, when "going viral" meant you needed to see a doctor. This was before some buffoon grabbing a local news reporter's microphone and shouting something obscene into the camera would end up on YouTube and get a bigger viewership than the news station had gotten that entire year. Even now, I don't understand the urge to go viral this way—not that there's a desirable way to go viral, let's be honest. But then, standing behind a news reporter meant, at the very best, you'd get twenty seconds of uninterrupted airtime blurring into the background.

But I suppose the idea of being on television was titillating, especially to a young, impressionable nerd like myself. Everybody watches TV! Being on TV automatically means you're famous! And being famous is basically the coolest thing in the world. It's the reason those annoying people at baseball games lose their shit whenever the camera pans to them for five seconds. It's the reason the entire city of Los Angeles exists. The magic of television.

. . .

I never thought I'd be on TV after that. In high school, I had a reputation for being a ticking time bomb of embarrassment. Whenever I'd raise my hand to answer a question, or more accurately, whenever I was called on to answer a question—I tried to avoid the spotlight as much as possible—it was only a matter of seconds before all of my blood rushed to my face and my cheeks turned an ungodly combination of beet red and fire. It would take at least another ten minutes for my face to return to normal. And this lasted well into college. In discussion sections—designed, I'm fairly certain, just so insufferable bros in beanies can philosophize about a book they've never read—I stuck faithfully to the minimum amount of participation required, and certainly never engaged in anything close to discussion. Honestly, I was sparing everybody the discomfort of having to be in the same room as someone who could turn as hideously scarlet as I could.

This is all to say that I never imagined myself on television, however enticing I found the idea of it, least of all as a nominee for a People's Choice Award for a series of videos I'd made for the Internet, and least of all as the unceremonious winner.

But I'm getting ahead of myself. Let's start from the beginning.

. . .

In the summer of 2014, I was working at the Internet company BuzzFeed, often characterized as a factory of lists, quizzes, and cat videos, which is not an entirely unfair portrait of what working at BuzzFeed was really like. It was a quintessentially millennial workspace, with all the clichés you can possibly imagine: a snack closet stocked with gluten-free candies and granola bars, a row of refrigerators full of seltzer water and beer, iced coffee on tap, visits from Internet-famous cats and one particularly adorable mini-horse named Mystic, and rows upon rows of young, talented, creative people.

My job, for better or worse, was to make stuff people would find funny and share with their friends. I wrote hundreds of lists and quizzes, and even curated my fair share of cat videos. At one point, I was officially listed as a senior editor on the Animals masthead, an accomplishment my journalism professors surely found worthwhile. About two years into my job there, I asked my boss if I could get drunk at lunch and review a One Direction album—trust me, I've had worse ideas—and she said yes. The drunk-at-work barrier officially broken, it was only a matter of time before I proposed getting drunk in the middle of the day and capturing the whole thing on camera.

Now, you might be wondering how someone who hated public speaking to the point of turning into a living beet-human would find himself in front of the camera, and the truth is, like all terrible things in life, because of karaoke. I'd never been a fan of karaoke. I found it terribly unpleasant. My first week at BuzzFeed—and my first ever week in New York City—there was a party to celebrate the launch of some new section of the website, and we all went to a karaoke bar near the office. I'd been to karaoke before, but always as an unwitting bystander, mumbling the words along with everybody else at an undetectable volume.

But this time was different. It was a small private room—one of the rooms where you can scream as obnoxiously as you want, only disturbing your closest friends instead of complete strangers. This night, everybody was wasted. Everybody was screaming along. Nobody could sing. Halfway through the night, the part of the night when everybody's eyes sort of glaze over, one of my new coworkers was on the tiny stage at the end of the room, crooning away, when another coworker got up behind him and started gyrating sensually to the music before taking something out of his pocket—a Mexican wrestling mask, it became apparent, as he unfolded it—and placed it on his head. "Weird," I thought, "but OK. I'm drunk. I can go along with this." And then, still gyrating to the music, he took off his shirt, and underneath, he was wearing a leather Princess Leia bra. It's unclear to me whether he'd slipped this on in the bathroom sometime in the last hour, or if he'd been wearing it the entire day, or if this was something he wore every day. I still have no idea. But what I do know is that I was utterly and completely baffled by everything I was seeing, and how normal everybody else considered what was happening.

Oh, that's just Gavin, someone explained when I asked

what the hell was going on, as if that should somehow satisfy my curiosity. But that night, I had one of those end-of-a-rom-com kind of moments, when time sort of slows down around you and the lights all fade together and you just kind of sit back and smile at how everything's played out, while everybody slowly dances around your head, gyrating in Princess Leia lingerie and *lucha libre* headgear. I don't even think I got up and sang that night, but it was one of those moments where I felt like I was among my people, where I could do anything and not feel embarrassed or ashamed.

After that evening, karaoke became a main staple of my idea of New York City nightlife. It took a while before I got comfortable enough to get onstage, but watching everybody else, how confident they were even when they could barely sing, was inspiring. When I finally did sing, I performed a stirring rendition of "And I Am Telling You" from the soundtrack to *Dreamgirls*, and the applause that I got after was one of the greatest feelings ever. Karaoke changed my worldview. "What's the worst that can happen, besides disappointing Jennifer Hudson?"

So, when on-camera work became a possibility at Buzz-Feed, I felt like I could do it, or at least try it. What's the worst that could happen? Besides disappointing Jennifer Hudson?

So we started filming a series of videos where I'd get drunk at my desk—an entire bottle of wine in only a few minutes—rant about one thing or another, then hastily edit a five-minute cut together, often still drunk, and post it to Facebook. In a matter of weeks, those videos got millions of views, and they soon became our very own version of must-see Internet. Karaoke on the biggest stage. Maybe not the biggest stage, but a much bigger one than I was used to. It was exciting but terrifying. Drunk moms from Minnesota started stopping me in the street. I was interviewed by a Canadian news station. It was all happening.

And then, one afternoon in late 2015—about a year into posting videos—I got a tweet from a random stranger asking if I knew I was nominated for a People's Choice Award. I had no idea. I didn't believe it. People tweet me a lot of shit, and of all the shit people have tweeted at me, nobody had ever asked if I was nominated for a People's Choice Award. I was understandably suspicious. But then I looked it up. And it was true! I was nominated for a People's Choice Award for favorite social media star. Granted, this was only the short list, some twenty people who *might* be nominated if all their followers voted for them, and the other people in my category were people who, in some cases, had tens of millions more followers than I had. There'd be no way in hell I'd make it beyond the short list. And sure, like they tell you, it's an honor just to be nominated—or short-listed—but nobody wants to be short-listed when they could win. I wanted to win.

But I'm not lying when I tell you I have no idea how the hell this shit works. Nobody tells you anything. I didn't even know I was on the short list until some random person on Twitter told me. They don't send you an e-mail saying, "Hey, this is how shit works." You just have to figure it all out yourself. But I made a half-assed effort to try to get people to vote for me. And they did.

A handful of weeks later, they announced the finalists. Some guy from some TV show that I've never watched got up to the little podium and read out the nominees for my category, and he mispronounced the hell out of my name, but he said my name! I was *officially* nominated! Not just a short-lister, but a full-blown, actually could maybe win this shit, will maybe get to go to the show in Hollywood nominee. If I died that night, no matter how grimly, my obituary would still cite me as "People's Choice Award Nominee Matt Bellassai." As in "People's Choice Award Nominee Matt Bellassai died today choking to death on an egg roll in his apartment. He was found peacefully at home, naked in bed, covered in duck sauce, watching homosexual pornography. He will be incinerated in a Krispy Kreme oven this Saturday and his ashes will be thrown at Beyoncé at her earliest possible convenience, as per his last will and testament."

For the weeks after that, I made a not-so-subtle effort for votes. But of course, there was no way of telling how well I was doing. One of the other nominees, a teen heartthrob with vague abs and a full head of hair, was trending worldwide on Twitter. No matter how many times my mother assured me she was voting, my efforts seemed futile. But I still campaigned till the very last moment.

I didn't hear anything for weeks, and I still had no idea what was going on. I didn't even know if I'd get to go to the awards show. I didn't know what dress I was wearing. I didn't know if I could bring a guest, or if alcohol would be provided or if I had to bring my own from home. But finally, I got word that I'd be attending the show—all the nominees were indeed invited—and I had only a few weeks to get myself to Los Angeles, get an outfit, and figure out the alcohol situation.

Now, I'm not a particular fan of Los Angeles as a city

or as a concept. I've been there countless times since then, but before the awards show, I'd only been once or twice and I hadn't gotten used to the city's bullshit. Of course, now I understand how to navigate the city: never make direct eye contact with anybody who's going or recently been to hot yoga, never agree to take a wheatgrass shot, and never disrespect In-N-Out, even though their french fries aren't even that good. Overall, though, it's too hot, there's too much traffic, and everybody is too beautiful for society to function properly. No community can ever last if everybody in it is beautiful all the time. No matter how much I love getting my Starbucks from a barista who looks exactly like Zac Efron, we need ugly people to balance out the world. That's just how it works. Besides, everybody in Los Angeles is certifiably insane. I had an Uber driver in L.A. who told me her ex-husband kidnapped her children, and before I had a chance to fully express my shock, she told me she was currently working on a screenplay about the entire incident, and every ounce of human emotion I had in that moment evaporated.

The week of the awards show, I had to find something to wear, and I went with someone from BuzzFeed to help me pick out the finest suit we could find at the Men's Wearhouse in L.A., and yes, before you question whether I'm telling the truth, let me assure you, I did actually wear a Men's Wearhouse suit to an awards show where I was nominated. Hollywood! You grow up watching televised award shows and assume everybody there is dressed in Versace that Donatella personally stitched onto each of their bodies, but the truth is, half the people at any given awards show—and there are hundreds of these things happening every week—are wearing a bargain dress from Sears and at least five layers of compression underwear. Unless you're Lady Gaga and show up with a team of specialists who pluck, pinch, and plaster over any semblance of what makes your body a normal human body, you're on your own. So yes, we picked out a fabulously gray Men's Wearhouse suit, the color of zombie skin, and paired it with a black shirt and gray-and-black plaid tie. I looked like a slightly more pampered version of a JCPenney store manager. Seriously, if I could go back and change anything about what happens in this entire chapter, I would change this outfit, and we haven't even gotten to the night of the awards show yet. It was that drab.

. . .

The day of the awards is an uncharacteristically gloomy day in Los Angeles, a wonderfully foreboding sign of what's to come. It's a Wednesday, and I assume they're holding it in the middle of the week to get a discount on the theater. Besides, Ellen DeGeneres will be there, and you're not getting Ellen to come out on a Friday night.

Around 11 a.m. is when the grooming starts, which is a ridiculously early and counterproductive time to start pampering yourself—I sweat through at least three layers of clothing before lunch on a normal day, how am I supposed to make it to the show in one piece if we start this early? But considering that every show taped on the West Coast is recorded for the East Coast prime time audience, everything in Los Angeles has to start three hours earlier than any normal human behavior.

Now, everybody at any event in Los Angeles is groomed to within an inch of their life. Men, women, children, dogs—half of them have their hair and makeup done just to go to Whole Foods, and frankly, considering everybody in that city is so horrifically gorgeous, I don't blame them. Whenever I'm in L.A., I try wearing the biggest pair of sunglasses to cover as much of my face as possible, to save myself the embarrassment of being compared to the natives. On a day like this, where there'll be cameras and lights and a red carpet, you better believe the bar is raised.

Fortunately, I was getting pampered. It's not my favorite thing in the world to have someone painting my face with makeup. I have a bad history with makeup. When I was five, my mother insisted on dressing me up as Frankenstein's monster for Halloween, a costume that seemed adorable, but required that she apply a thick layer of chalky green makeup to my face every time we needed to pose for pictures. I hated the smell of that makeup. It smelled of melted Tupperware full of old chili, and she absolutely refused to let me wear the costume without the face of makeup. But every time she tried to apply it to my face, I'd start violently gagging and thrashing, and the tears would streak through the makeup, and any bit of it that she would manage to get on my face would be smeared off in seconds anyway. There is no existing picture of this Halloween that doesn't feature my tear-streaked face.

But it's a lot easier to get through the makeup process when you're twenty-five and can legally be wasted during it. And besides, on this day, I was getting the good stuff. BuzzFeed was paying for everything, or rather, BuzzFeed *had* to pay for everything, because I didn't have any money. To be honest, I'm not entirely sure what I would've done without a company like BuzzFeed—you can be nominated for an award, and you still gotta fly yourself to the city it's in, get yourself a hotel room, get an outfit, hair, makeup, shoes, transportation to the venue, a male prostitute to keep you warm that night. It's a whole big deal. But I guess that's what credit cards are for.

There was a brief hiccup when the hairstylist decided to give me 2004 Green Day emo throwback comb-over bangs, but we managed to course-correct soon enough.

I squeezed myself into my hideous suit and finally hopped into a van with my entourage—a BuzzFeed publicist (there to ensure that I didn't embarrass the company, I'm sure), me, and my date for the evening, Jeremy, a video producer who'd helped create the mess that got us there in the first place.

When you pull up to an awards show, it's absolute chaos. After the initial shock hits that you're on a red carpet, just like on TV, and there's lights and cameras and beautiful people wearing horrifying amounts of bronzer, you start to realize that there's absolutely no order or reason to what is happening. I imagine this is what animals who have been held in captivity feel like when they're released back into the wild. There's a faint sense of familiarity to everything—these are human beings with faces and limbs, I recognize those things—but everything else is sheer pandemonium. Or at least controlled pandemonium.

When you get out of the car, it's like getting onto the world's worst conveyer belt. You're whisked into a tent and along a path, through a security checkpoint where a guard with a gun judges you when you empty your pockets and all that's inside is lip gloss and oil-blotting sheets. Once you're deemed safe, you step right onto the stretch of carpet where attendees stop and pose for photographers, before taking another ten steps and then stopping again, and so on and so forth until everybody dies a fiery death. There's no order to it, at least not at the People's Choice Awards, so the sequence of people walking along the carpet is simply the sequence of people who happened to arrive at that very moment, and in this very moment, I happen to be sandwiched between Kate Hudson and Jack Black. And let me tell you, photographers don't give a shit about you, especially when someone more famous is within five feet of where you're standing. But that doesn't change the order of things! So then you're walking along the carpet and photographers are shouting at you, but not as loud as they're shouting at Kate Hudson and Jack Black. You can feel the corners of your mouth shaking, partly because your cheeks are starting to ache from smiling, but partly because you're afraid your bangs fell back to Green Day status. A typical photographer interaction goes like this:

"Who are you?!"

"I'm Matt."

"What do you do?!"

"Um. I write stuff on the Internet."

At this point, the photographer's face always drops. "Oh."

"I'm nominated for an award," I shouted at one of them in indignation.

And then, "Fine. Look over here. And try not to look like you're shitting your pants!"

OK, nobody actually said that. But they might as well have.

When the photographer stands end, someone pushes you out of the way to make room for Jack Black, and the conveyer belt continues. The next part of the carpet is where all the press stands waiting with lights, cameras, and microphones, craning their necks to see who's coming along the carpet. Typically, this is the part where your publicist walks ahead of you, goes up to some of the reporters, and says, "I have Matt Bellassai, the guy with the wine," and the reporters will shrug their shoulders and shake their heads. Typically, your publicist will try to get far enough ahead of you so that you don't have to bear witness to this rejection firsthand, but the carpet is far too crowded for you to stray too far without getting lost, so you hear all of it. Nobody wants to talk to an Internet writer when Kate Hudson just walked through.

And of course, I was well prepared for this part of the carpet. After all, I was a writer at BuzzFeed for a couple of years before then, and had found myself on the other side of the carpet rope plenty of times, waiting for one celebrity or another to walk by so I could scream their name and pray they'd stop and give me some innocuous quote. I'd had plenty of hapless publicists come up to me and whisper, "I have *so-and-so*, from *so-and-so*," and I'd shyly wag my head and shrug my shoulders and hope that they didn't take it personally. It's all part of the never-ending fuck-fest that is Hollywood. But the conveyer belt plugs along regardless of your feelings. After getting rejected by one too many people with microphones, you're pushed through another tent and then a walkway and then someone is scanning your ticket and handing you a badge and you're shoved inside the theater like cattle shoved into a slaughter truck. The conveyer belt has ended, and somehow, you've survived.

. . .

We finally got inside the venue, and honestly I don't even remember what series of hallways and entrances we walked through to get backstage, but the event staff led us to a tiny greenroom where we could hang out before the show started. Now, at this point, I'd seen plenty of celebrities who had, at some time or another, made their way to BuzzFeed for photographs or interviews. I wouldn't consider myself a person easily star-stricken, no matter how much I fawn over my favorite celebrities on Twitter. But on this night, I was seriously bugging out. Because this greenroom was literally the holding room for every single celebrity who was there that night. On one couch sat the entire cast of *Grey's Anatomy*—and sure, that show has been on since the dawn of time, but still, I'd certainly never been in the same room with any of them. In one corner there was Sandra Bullock and Melissa McCarthy and all of the hot people from those CW shows whose names I can never remember but whose abs I've seen on the Internet. In another corner stood Chris Hemsworth, in all his meaty glory, and had I not been so deliriously paralyzed by everything that was happening, I would've taken a handful of him. But too much was happening all at once. All I could think to do was ask a person with a staff badge where, perhaps, I could find some alcohol, and she looked at me with eyes that suggested she thought I'd somehow snuck inside, before telling me that there was no alcohol backstage. But in any case, the show was starting in only a few minutes, and we had to find our seats inside the theater.

Of course, when you walk into any theater in Los Angeles, especially when you haven't gotten used to this kind of thing, you sort of lose your breath. It's almost impossible to tell who's famous and who's just a really ridiculously good-looking person, but I didn't have much time to process everything around me because the show was starting and an army of producers in headsets were barking at everybody to find their seats, sit down, and shut up.

I sat in awe as the show progressed, and one celebrity after another came onstage. We were only a few rows from the front, and could see where each person was sitting, who they were talking to, how nervous they looked before they went onstage (the gratifying thing about Hollywood: nobody knows what the hell they're doing, except maybe Oprah, and everybody is nervous as hell). Meanwhile, every three minutes, my parents would text me from their viewing party at home to tell me that they caught a glimpse of my face as the camera panned over the crowd.

Beforehand, the producers told us that my category wouldn't be announced onstage. Here's a not-so-secret secret about award shows: nobody gives a fuck about the awards. Everybody is here for the glamour and the cameras and the spectacle. The People's Choice Awards give out something like sixty awards every year, and only about fifteen of them are handed out onstage to people like Ellen and Selena Gomez who are actually famous and not just on the Internet. But the producers did tell us that they would hand out the award in the audience just when they came back from a commercial break, and they would give us a heads-up when that was about to happen. Otherwise, all we had to do was sit and chill.

Commercial breaks during award shows are absolute anarchy. The second the cameras turn off for a commercial, about half of the room stands up and shuffles about, going to the bathroom, heading backstage for a snack, or ditching the show entirely because they've seen what they came for and they're fucking sick of it. An army of seat-fillers—a bunch of hot young aspiring actors and actresses who want to be around famous people—come in and fill all of the empty seats so that when the cameras return, they return to a nice, big room, full of beautiful people who definitely didn't just play the biggest, most celebrity-filled game of musical chairs. The last thirty seconds before they come back from commercial is like a scene from a war movie, with producers running up and down the aisles, screaming at everything with a face, shoving every warm body into any available seat, skipping over rolls and rolls of camera cord, and elbowing production interns in the head. Honestly, I'm pretty sure I remember seeing one of them pull a gun and shoot an assistant in the neck. It's an absolutely glorious mess, and twice as entertaining as the actual show.

About halfway through the evening, during one of the commercial breaks, just as the cameras shut off, a producer runs up to me, trailed by a cameraman. She leans in.

"You're Matt Balthazar, right?" she shouts.

"Um. Matt Bellassai? Yeah, that's me."

She shouts again, "OK, good, we wanted to make sure you're in your seat. Get ready."

At this point, my heart is pounding, or at least beating as hard as it can beneath the layers of Spanx I'm wearing. I mean, she's making sure I'm in the right seat, she's saying "get ready," that's gotta be a good sign, right?

She goes back to the cameraman a few rows in front of us and points to me. The cameraman cranes his neck around the camera to get a look at me, he points at me to make sure he has the right fat, balding ginger, and the producer nods.

I'm freaking out. My stomach is churning. I'm sweating through my disgusting Men's Wearhouse suit because their cheap fabrics aren't breathable enough to handle my superhuman levels of body humidity.

We hear someone shout, "THIRTY SECONDS TO AIR," and everybody starts moving in different directions. Producers are screaming into microphones, hustling people this way and that way, barking orders at everyone in sight. "TEN SECONDS," someone else shouts, and the final chaotic dash for open seats commences. In the aisle where I'm sitting a woman in a dress appears holding a glistening award statue. None of the other nominees in my category are sitting nearby, which can only mean one thing. I prepare my least nervous smile. I get ready to act surprised, to wave to the camera in glee as I hoist my award—*my* award!—to the sky.

"FIVE. FOUR. THREE . . ."

And just as the cameras get ready to blaze back to life, just as the audience roars back to on-air applause, a seat-filler—some woman in tacky heels and a tight black dress—rushes in front of the camera to try jumping into a seat in the row directly in front of us. The producer's veins bulge from her neck as she screams, "GET OUT OF THE

WAY! GET OUT OF THE WAY!" But people are standing to make room for the woman in the black dress to sit. Everybody finally lowers to their seats, but by then, the cameraman is already moving forward, and in the confusion, he stops on the man sitting directly in front of me. And for a moment, time stops entirely.

I should point out, for the record, that the man sitting in front of me looks absolutely nothing like me. I could understand, even sympathize with the cameraman—the very same cameraman who had pointed directly at me seconds earlier—had the man in front of me been wearing glasses, or had a comb-over, or was wearing a similarly appalling Men's Wearhouse suit hastily purchased the day before. But none of these things was true. The man in front of me had jet-black hair, a beard, and giant, gleaming teeth, and to top it all off, he was approximately thirty-five years older than me. And sure, maybe that cameraman suffers from one of those diseases where you can't tell faces apart, or maybe he had recently sustained one of those debilitating injuries to the part of the brain that remembers things for longer than five seconds, but in either case, I might kindly suggest that he pursue a different line of work until he's able to correctly distinguish an overweight bespectacled ginger from an old coot with fluorescent teeth. But now we'll never know.

I look sidewise at Jeremy beside me and chuckle nervously. It's the only thing I can do.

Meanwhile, the cameraman is screaming now. "You won!" he screams at the man in front of me. "Act excited!"

The man in front of me, just as confused as the rest of us, of course, gives the camera two thumbs-up and smiles wildly. On the jumbo screens above us, the man is grinning frantically, and below his face it says "MATT BELLASSAI, Favorite Social Media Star."

Behind the cameraman, all the while, the producer is hysterically waving her hands. "NOT HIM!" she's shouting in vain, pulling at her hair. "NOT HIM!" But everything around us is too loud, the cameraman can't hear, and the man in front of me is waving too wildly for anybody to care.

The woman with the statue comes forward and hands the award to me, but it's too late. The cameraman is already moving back up the aisle to his next shot, and the producer is following, shaking her head behind him. The lights are dimming. Flames are shooting from the stage. The music begins to blare. And Jason Derulo walks out to thunderous applause.

It's all over in about twenty seconds.

. . .

The moments afterward are still a little blurry, in no small part because Jason Derulo was screaming onstage. I believe the first words that came out of my mouth afterward were "What the *fuck* just happened?" Jeremy's mouth hung open and he started nervously laughing beside me. "Dude," he said, "I have no idea." His concern in that moment, I imagine, was making sure I didn't run directly into Jason Derulo's flames. "That . . . was a mess," he said. And then I think I said something like "I want to use this award to bash someone's head in."

And yes, to be perfectly fair, they did hand it to me and

it *did* have my name on it—all very exciting, I won! I got to take it home!—but it was also quite heavy and in that moment, I thought, it would have made the perfect blunt object with which to smash a certain cameraman's soft skull.

Soon enough, my phone started buzzing as people expressed a combination of elation and mourning, like I'd just won a brand-new puppy that someone subsequently stabbed to death in front of me. "Sorry, dude, that sucks," one friend texted me. "But at least you won!" And then from my mother: "We still love you." As if the entire incident had cast their love in doubt, however briefly.

The next commercial break, as chaos broke out again, a different producer came to see me and asked if I wanted to go backstage and talk to the press. That's what all winners do, typically when they walk offstage—you go to a room back-stage and the press asks you dumb questions like, "How does it feel to win?"

"Um. Sure, I guess," I told him. I still barely knew what was going on. My heart was still beating violently in my chest.

The producer led me backstage, back through the doors we'd entered to take our seats, back through the hallway past the holding room. The producer is a few feet ahead of me, and as we walk through a door, another staffer stops me and says, "Do you have a badge to be back here?"

And this, I admit, was my most aggressive diva moment of the night. Because in that moment, I held up the statue with my name on it, looked that wretched staffer directly in the face, and shouted, "DOES THIS COUNT!?"

And I'll concede, it felt damned good. Almost as good

as I imagine it would have felt to smash in that cameraman's head.

But then she was like, "No. It doesn't. Do you have a badge?" The producer who'd been leading me realizes I'm not behind him anymore and comes back to fetch me. "He's with me," he tells the door staffer. And the door staffer is like, "I don't care. He needs a badge."

So I had to stand there like a fool, shamefully digging into the pockets of my wilting Men's Wearhouse suit for the badge I'd stuffed in one of them an hour before. Meanwhile, Sharon Osbourne walks past us, no badge—and no award (just saying)—while I'm furiously reaching into my jacket for a hint of plastic. Finally, I dig out the badge and I'm like, "HERE. ARE YOU HAPPY?!" And she waves me through like nothing happened.

When I get to the pressroom, someone shouted for me to stand in the corner while they stuck a camera in my face. I had absolutely no idea what was happening. I held up my award and forced an awkward smile and gave a tiny uncomfortable wave. The camera lingered for what felt like ten whole minutes, then disappeared. That footage, I'd learn after, would be aired later in the show to make up for the mistake, but hilariously, in the background, you can hear someone say, "Who's he?" And someone else replies, "No idea."

A man in a suit and white-blond hair approached me and shook my hand. "Congratulations," he said with a laugh. He introduced himself as the president of the People's Choice Awards—yes, there's a president of the People's Choice Awards.

"Do you know what happened out there?" he asked me.

I laughed at first, because I thought he was joking, but

then I realized he was seriously asking me if I knew what just happened.

"Yes?" I said. "The camera was on the wrong person."

"Did you plan that?" he asked me.

"What do you mean?" I asked back. In my head, I was thinking, "What the fuck are you talking about? This is your show!"

"Oh," he said. "We thought maybe you told the camera guy to do that."

I'm sure my mouth was gaping, because he patted me on the shoulder, said something like "Well, sorry about that, but congrats anyway," and walked away, leaving me to figure out what the hell I was supposed to do next.

A backstage producer came up to me and asked, in the same tone that you ask a child you've found lost in a grocery store, "Would you like to find your publicist?" And I nodded my head sheepishly, so we tracked down Liz, the BuzzFeed publicist, who similarly greeted me like a child she'd lost at a grocery store and looked at me with a searching gaze, trying to detect what mood I was in, whether I found this all hilarious or maddening or both.

"What the fuck happened?" she asked me, and I was like, "I still have no idea. I just want alcohol."

She led me farther backstage, where a row of photographers took the obligatory pictures of me holding my award. I'm clearly sweating my face off in all of those photos, and my smile looks like the smile of a person who just strangled a man in a motel shower, but what beautiful memories I'll have forever.

Afterward, we walked back to the greenroom. There was

still no alcohol there, just Sharon Osbourne and a platter of brownies. I can't be positive, but I'm pretty sure I ate approximately seventy of those brownies in that moment.

To top it all off, John Stamos—who'd won for some show he was in—walked into the greenroom and went to set down his own award next to mine. And I said something like, "Uh-oh, we don't wanna mix those up," and he looked at me, dead serious, and said, "You can have mine." But then he smiled that Uncle Jesse smile, even though I was already furiously stuffing his award into my back pocket. And I would've gotten away with it, too, if it wasn't for my goddamn Men's Wearhouse suit.

·   ·   ·

When everything finally died down, Jeremy and I went to the after-party. The heads of the accounting firm that tabulates the results of the awards—those people you always see on television carrying the suitcases—came up to me while I was double-fisting champagne with my award under my armpit (yeah, you just have to carry it with you the rest of the night) and apologized for the mix-up, but they assured me the results were all very real and I'd really, truly won the thing, which in some small way was a genuine comfort, since a part of me assumed they had only picked me out of pity over my laughable chances. I told them thank you between mouthfuls of appetizers, and we all took a lovely picture together that I'm sure exists somewhere in the universe.

At this point, it was still only 8 p.m., but I was physically exhausted, and the only real famous person at the after-party was celebrity attorney Gloria Allred, so Jeremy and I left.

On the way back to the hotel, we stopped and got tacos, and I dragged those tacos back to my hotel bed and ate them in my underwear with my award cradled beside me. And yes, I kissed her good night. And tucked her in. And was glad she was covered in taco grease, and not the juices of a cameraman's skull.

. . .

The next day, I got a text message from a number I didn't recognize, from a man named Eric who introduced himself as the man with the teeth who was sitting in front of me the night before. He asked if he could call me, and a few minutes later, we were on the phone together.

"I'm so sorry about what happened," he told me. "I wasn't even supposed to be in the audience, but I'm a vocal coach, and Jason is one of my students."

Jason, I realize, was Jason Derulo.

"He was performing and he wanted me in the audience to watch him," he said. "I had no idea why the cameras were on me, but they told me to smile!"

I assured him he did nothing wrong, it was the cameraman's fault! And then I made him promise to give me vocal lessons. Because if this ever happens again, I sure as hell better be able to sing my way out of it.

acknowledgments

Sorry to my editor, Jhanteigh Kupihea, for missing just about every single deadline she assigned to me, for testing her abundant patience, and for mounting a serious campaign against her optimism. I hope I haven't broken you completely. I understand if you have a voodoo doll made in my image and pierce it in the eye every single night. Honestly, if you don't have one, I'd be disappointed.

Sorry to my literary agent, Cait Hoyt, for making you wonder whether I'd just been napping every time you tried to call me. (I was. I was napping every time.) She remains the only agent whose office I've nearly cried in, and I would be scared of her if she didn't pay for every dinner we've ever eaten together. I'm convinced she would kill someone if I asked her. She probably already has.

Sorry to the entire team at Keywords Press, Atria, and Simon & Schuster, for all of my e-mails, questions, notes, and last-minute revisions. Sorry to Loan Le for having to decipher my e-mails to find the part where I was asking for more time past a deadline. Sorry to Ariele Fredman for all of my publicity demands, which include selling this book as a Happy Meal toy in every McDonald's around the country. It's a great idea and you should reconsider, if only for our nation's youth.

Sorry to Koury Angelo and his amazing team for having to take photos of my face eating cold pasta, takeout noodles, and french fries for five hours. And sorry to Albert Tang and the rest of the design team at Simon & Schuster for having to look at all those pictures and turn them into an actual book cover. Sorry to everyone else who worked on my book, including Judith Curr, Jackie Jou, Kimberly Goldstein, Chelsea Cohen, and Dana Sloan.

Sorry to my own team, past and present, for making you check on me every day to make sure I hadn't thrown myself off a bridge in the middle of writing this book, and also for everything else. Sorry to Courtney and Ashley for the fight I put up while they tried to convince me to take a chance on myself. Sorry to Vanessa, Adam, Andy, Andrew, Matt, Tess, Alexandra, Nora, Luke, and Josh for being a general pain in the ass.

Sorry to Harry Styles, Chris Hemsworth, Chris Evans, Chris Pine, Liam Hemsworth, the guy from the Trivago commercials, Zac Efron, Taylor Lautner, Tyler Posey, Daniel Radcliffe, John Boyega, Nick and Joe Jonas but not the third one, Tom Daley, Jake Gyllenhaal, Oscar Isaac, Eddie Redmayne, Rami Malek, Bradley Cooper, Prince Harry, all the guys from *Game Of Thrones*, Ryan Gosling, Henry Cavill, John Legend, David Beckham, Idris Elba, Alexander Skarsgård, Matt Bomer, and Jamie Dornan for harassing you on the Internet.

Sorry to my friends for the anxiety I brought to the bar because I was supposed to be writing instead of drinking.

And most of all, sorry to my family—Mom, Dad, Anthony, cousins, aunts, uncles, grandparents—for subjecting you to almost three decades of my awkwardness and then turning you all into stories. I should've told you sooner that loving me came with a price.